Are We Still a Nation at Risk Two Decades Later?

William Hayes

ScarecrowEducation
Lanham, Maryland • Toronto • Oxford
2004

Published in the United States of America
by ScarecrowEducation
An imprint of The Rowman & Littlefield Publishing Group, Inc.
4501 Forbes Boulevard, Suite 200, Lanham, Maryland 20706
www.scaroweducation.com

PO Box 317
Oxford
OX2 9RU, UK

British Library Cataloguing in Publication Information Available

Library of Congress Cataloging-in-Publication Data

Hayes, William, 1938–
    Are we still a nation at risk two decades later? / William Hayes.
        p. cm.
    Includes bibliographical references and index.
    ISBN 1-57886-179-9 (pbk. : alk. paper)
    1. Education and state—United States. 2. Educational change—United
States. 3. United States. National Commission on Excellence in Education.
Nation at risk. I. Title.
    LC89.H39 2004
    379.73—dc22

                                                                2004012446

Contents

Acknowledgments

I am deeply indebted to Chelsea Durham, a sophomore in the Teacher Education program at Roberts Wesleyan and a student worker in the division office. Chelsea has been more than a typist. She has been involved in every aspect of the book. In addition, my wife Nancy has been not only a proofreader but has made valuable suggestions that have improved the final text. Chelsea and Nancy deserve much of the credit for this book, and I am extremely grateful to them both for their help and patience during this project. It could not have been done without them.

Preface

There is widespread agreement among those who have studied the history of education in the United States that the publication of the *A Nation at Risk* report in 1983 was instrumental in creating a significant school reform movement during the last two decades. Respected historian, Diane Ravitch, wrote in a recent book which traced educational reform during the twentieth century that:

> *A Nation at Risk* was a landmark of education reform literature. Countless previous reports by prestigious national commissions had been ignored by the national press and the general public. *A Nation at Risk* was different. Written in stirring language that the general public could understand, the report warned that schools had not kept pace with the changes in society and the economy and that the nation would suffer if education were not dramatically improved for all children. It also asserted that lax academic standards were correlated with lax behavior standards and that neither should be ignored. *A Nation at Risk* was a call to action.[1]

In *Critical Issues on Education*, a book used as a textbook in many college education programs, the authors assert, "The 1983 publication of *A Nation at Risk* was the catalyst for today's standards-based reform movement."[2] Another popular textbook used in preparing future teachers compares the impact of the report to that of the results of the Russian launch of Sputnik in 1957.

> *A Nation at Risk*, issued by the National Commission on Excellence in Education, had an impact similar to that of Sputnik in 1957. The report

made a strong case for the urgency of reform if the nation was to retain its place in the modern world. It was followed by a myriad of other studies and reports, but there is no question that *A Nation at Risk* had the most influence.[3]

In the book *School*, a publication which accompanied a four-part public television series, the authors wrote that the *A Nation at Risk* report "crystallized the growing sense of unease with public schooling in the business community by tightly coupling mediocre economic performance in the global marketplace."[4]

What was it that made this report, which was one of many issued during the 1980s, so influential? Certainly one factor was that it was written in a style that was uncluttered by educational jargon. Its widely quoted introduction has been reprinted in newspapers, periodicals, and books. This paragraph in the strongest terms stated that our educational system was truly in trouble and, as a result, it captured the attention of readers as it claimed that

> our Nation is at risk. Our once unchallenged prominence in commerce, industry, science, and technological innovation is being overtaken by competitors throughout the world. . . . If an unfriendly foreign power had attempted to impose on America the mediocre educational performance that exists today, we might well have viewed it as an act of war. As it stands, we have allowed this to happen to ourselves. We have even squandered the gains in student achievement made in the wake of the Sputnik challenge. Moreover, we have dismantled essential support systems, which helped make those gains possible. We have, in effect, been committing an act of unthinking, unilateral educational disarmament.[5]

Even these stirring and alarming words would not have had such an impact if the nation's citizens were not already concerned about their schools. In 1983, there were also underlying fears in the nation brought about by an economy that seemed to be becoming much less competitive in the world market. Some Americans were wondering what had gone wrong.

This report galvanized some Americans, moving education to center stage. Remember, in 1983, we were in two wars: the Cold War with the Soviet Union and an economic war with Japan. Our national security was at stake, and poor school performance was putting the nation at risk.[6]

The purpose of this book is to first examine why and how this report was written. After summarizing the findings of the Commission, which prepared the final recommendations, there is an analysis of the views of those who have criticized the report. A major portion of the book is devoted to examining and evaluating the educational reforms that can be traced directly to the recommendations put forward in the study. Finally, there is an attempt to assess the historical impact of the report after more than twenty years and to describe the current status of education in the United States. There is no question that many problems remain and that new ones have become evident. As we face the challenges of ensuring excellence in our educational system, one is reminded of the words of John Gardner when he said, "We are all faced with a series of great opportunities brilliantly disguised as unsolvable problems."[7] This book does not offer definitive solutions to all of these "unsolvable problems" in American education, but hopefully it identifies and illuminates the "great opportunities" that the future offers.

NOTES

1. Diane Ravitch, *Left Back: A Century of Battles Over School Reform* (New York: Touchstone, 2000), 411–12.

2. Jack L. Nelson, Stuart B. Palonsky, and Mary Rose McCarthy, *Critical Issues in Education: Dialogues and Dialectics* (Boston: McGraw-Hill, 2000), 152.

3. John D. Pulliam and James Van Patten, *History of Education in America* (Upper Saddle River, NJ: Prentice-Hall, 1999), 242–43.

4. Sarah Mondale and Sarah B. Patton, eds., *School* (Boston: Beacon Press, 2001), 177.

5. Myra Pollack Sadker and David Miller Sadker, *Teachers, Schools, and Society* (Boston: McGraw-Hill, 2000), 148–49.

6. Sadker and Sadker, *Teachers, Schools, and Society*, 149.

7. John W. Gardner, www.thinkexist.com/English/Author/x/Author_4817_1 .htm (accessed 5 July 2003).

CHAPTER 1

The Beginning

In an address to the nation in July 1979, which the press labeled the "malaise speech," then President Jimmy Carter talked of "a crisis in confidence . . . that strikes at the soul and spirit of our national will."[1] Indeed there were serious problems facing the nation as we began the 1980s. Historian Harold Evans begins his chapter on the Reagan Revolution with these words:

> At the end of the seventies, America simmered with accumulated fears and frustrations. The country seemed ripe for political revolution. Middle-class families were already worried about rising unemployment and street crime, permissiveness and race relations.[2]

There were indeed problems on many fronts. During the presidential debates in 1980, Ronald Reagan asked the nation the very pointed question, "Are you happier today than when Mr. Carter became president?"[3] In December of 1981, 59 percent of the voters answered "no" to this question. In large part, this was the result of the dismal economic conditions in the nation. During the first year of the Reagan presidency, the national unemployment rate reached 10.7 percent, placing it at the highest level since the 1930s. Bankruptcies and farm foreclosures increased. Even though the economy was lagging, the inflation rate stood at 12.5 percent. To control the escalating cost of living, the Federal Reserve raised the prime interest rate to an alarming 21.5 percent.[4] The economic situation was unique in American history as economists and political leaders searched for remedies for what was labeled as "stagflation."

To face this crisis, Ronald Reagan brought to Washington the spirit of optimism and idealism. In contrast to President Carter, he appeared cheerfully confident that all of the problems could be solved, suggesting, "I find no malaise. . . . I find nothing wrong with the American people."[5]

The economy was just one of the many problems facing the United States. A significant number of people were extremely critical of what was happening in our schools. Some of the most vocal individuals came from the business community. They complained of inferior graduates who were ill-prepared to face the challenging jobs in our technological society. Many of these outspoken critics concluded that our poor education system was a major factor in our competitive business losses to other nations, especially the Japanese. Entering the 1980s, the business community saw our country losing the advantage in the automobile industry, the steel industry, and other technological areas.

Beyond the concerns with the economy, there were other reasons to worry about public education. In the book *Left Back*, Ravitch argues that

> By the early 1980s there was growing concern about the quality of the nation's schools. The sustained assault on the academic curriculum in the late 1960s and early 1970s had taken its toll. In 1980, the Gannett newspaper chain sent investigative reporters into twenty-two schools in nine states, where they discovered that academic credit was offered for such courses as cheerleading, student government, and mass media. In the average school, students had only three hours each day of instructional time; students spent most of their time, even in their academic classes, on nonacademic activities.[6]

There is little question that during the 1960s, especially in high schools, there were a number of changes. Like the colleges, high schools made a conscious effort to accommodate the increasing student pressure for increased "relevance" in the curriculum. As a result, many schools added numerous electives to their program. History in some cases was sacrificed to specific classes in political science, economics, sociology, or psychology. Classes were added in fields such as ecology, drama, and dance. At the same time, an increasing number of students spent a significant amount of their time during high school studying vocational skills ranging from beautician training to auto mechanics. Pressure from parents and other community groups pushed schools into creating mandated health education programs that taught topics such as sex education, the danger of drugs and alcohol, and nutrition.

Also, schools at all levels were affected by pressures to help students develop self-esteem. One of the tenets of the popular movement to establish middle schools was to assist students in the transition from the comfortable elementary school environment to the impersonal atmosphere of our high schools. Some of these schools appeared to sacrifice academic achievement for middle school students in order to achieve a more effective adjustment to the pressures of high school.

As the nation entered the 1980s, great importance was given to extracurricular activities in American high schools. A typical student might spend fifteen hours a week participating in an interscholastic athletic program while they would spend less time studying English and math combined. Clubs ranging from student council to the chess club maintained a high level of support among students, parents, and educators.

With all of these additional responsibilities taken on by the school, the time allotted for active instruction had, if anything, decreased. The 180 days, which make up most school calendars, frequently included a number of days when regular classes did not meet. Instruction days were used for teacher-training days, student testing, and parent-teacher conferences. Attempts to increase instruction time were very controversial, as faculty unions usually insisted on additional compensation. It was also true that parents and students reacted negatively to suggestions that the number of school days should be increased. Even attempts to lengthen the school day were met with spirited opposition. Such proposed changes often led to complaints from coaches and athletic directors because of the reduced time available for the teams to practice.

By 1980 there seemed to be a general feeling in the public and in the education profession that many students were not being challenged academically. While most high schools did have a college entrance program, there were many other possible majors, which included courses in business education, art, or music. These students might have only a minimal number of courses in history, English, math, or science. Foreign language was usually not required for the students who were taking any program other than college entrance. Because many colleges did not require it, even college-bound students frequently graduated without taking a foreign language. It was not unusual that students would take only one course in high school math and science. Even these classes might be watered down and called "Consumer Math" or "Physical Science."

At the elementary level there were problems as well. Based on the British model, a number of school districts attempted to establish open schools. School districts attempting to give additional flexibility to their programs built schools with large open spaces in which students were allowed additional freedom. This was even done at the secondary level. For most it proved a mistake as teachers erected barriers around their classroom space to ensure at least a minimal amount of privacy for their classes.

There were also spirited curriculum debates occurring in school districts throughout the nation. New ways of teaching math and reading divided the educational community during the 60s and 70s. An almost warlike intensity evolved between the advocates of whole language and those who supported the traditional phonics-based reading instruction. This conflict, like the "new math" of a previous decade, caused confusion for students, parents, and teachers alike.

Changes in classroom management procedure had also affected the school environment as corporal punishment was being eliminated as an alternative. Administrators attempted to create more "student-friendly" environments in the hope that it would reduce discipline problems. During the early 70s, dress codes for students and teachers were disappearing. Some schools even experimented with smoking lounges for high school students. Others went so far as to create an open campus where students could leave school grounds during their free periods or spend time in student lounges. Students were made part of the decision-making groups in districts as they were elected to a principal's advisory committee or even as a nonvoting member of the Board of Education. For many adults, some of these trends were alarming, and as a result the country was ripe for a movement, which would be labeled "back to basics."

During the entire twentieth century, the emphasis in our schools had moved like a pendulum between those who support student-centered learning for critical thinking and those who believe that the primary function of schools must be to teach the basic content and skills in the subjects of English, math, science, history, and foreign language. The introduction of progressive education by John Dewey and others at the beginning of the century began a debate that continues into the twenty-first century. The student-centered learning emphasis so evident in some schools during the 60s and 70s was seen by many Americans as a failure in 1980.

As a result, it is not surprising that there would be a swing back toward a more academic curriculum. This feeling is expressed in these words from the book *Critical Issues in Education*:

> the idea of liberal arts education for all slowly fell out of fashion after the first two decades of the twentieth century, as the pervasive influence of "progressive" education began to take hold. Since then, the story of American public schools has largely been the story of content-light education.[7]

In the same vein, prominent educational critic E. D. Hirsh has argued that

> the common knowledge characteristically shared by those at the top of the socioeconomic ladder in the United States should be readily available to all citizens because people who lack it suffer serious handicaps. This "core knowledge" is needed for productive communication and in establishing fundamental equality as citizens. That is the content of basic education and should be the primary focus of schooling.[8]

Despite the growing support for traditional academic learning, there were then and are now those who disagree. Perhaps one of the most articulate critics of the "back to basics" movement is John Holt, who has written that

> behind much of what we do in school lie some ideas that could be expressed roughly as follows: (1) Of the vast body of human knowledge, there are certain bits and pieces that can be called essential . . . ; (2) the extent to which a person can be considered educated . . . depends on the amount of this essential knowledge that he carries about with him; (3) it is the duty of the schools, therefore, to get as much of this essential knowledge as possible into the minds of children. . . . These ideas are absurd and harmful nonsense. . . . Children quickly forget all but a small part of what they learn in school. It is of no use or interest to them; they do not want, or expect, or even intend to remember it. The only difference between bad and good students in this respect is that the bad students forget right away, while the good students are careful to wait until after the exam.[9]

It could be said that the pendulum in the 1960s had swung in the direction of John Holt's point of view. One can read too much into such an assertion as it is equally true that schools have perhaps changed less during the twentieth century than most of our other institutions. If an older American were to visit a typical high school they would still find predominantly teacher-centered lessons most often taught using similar methods to the way they were taught as students.

Change in our public schools does not come easily. In part, this is true because of the way our schools are governed. All levels of government have a hand in managing our schools. Educational policy is affected by the courts, state legislatures, the national government, and local boards of education. Policy decisions are also susceptible to numerous pressure groups ranging from teachers' unions to the Parent Teacher Association (PTA). As a result, making a change even in the school calendar would arouse concerns about federal and state financial aid, the impact on students, families, faculty, and even school staff. Especially powerful in affecting decisions in school districts are the teachers' unions. Because of the many interested parties and the fact that power is divided between different levels of government, major change has been slow. What tends to happen is that on a number of issues, there is limited movement between the ideas of the progressives and the traditionalists.

For the majority of Americans in 1980, there was an underlying feeling that we needed to return to emphasizing the basic academic disciplines. Certainly Ronald Reagan and his closest supporters spoke frequently about the need to move toward basic education. At the same time, the new president and his Republican Party did not feel that the federal government had any significant responsibility in the field of public education. The Republican Party platform in 1980 actually called for dismantling the federal Department of Education. President Jimmy Carter, in 1979, had just created a cabinet-level position and appointed the first Secretary of Education. His stated purpose in doing so was to give public education a more prominent place on our nation's social agenda. The previous organizational pattern had been to combine health, education, and welfare into one federal department with a single cabinet secretary. Because the leadership of the Republican Party at that time saw education as the primary responsibility of state and local government, it was their opinion that the cabinet-level post merely added to an already bloated and wasteful bureaucracy. It should be noted that President Reagan was a man who often suggested that the federal government does not solve problems, but is the problem.

With this point of view, one would not have expected the Reagan administration to create a movement that would bring about major changes in the schools of this country. Despite the lack of a strong federal commitment to change schools, President Reagan's Department of Education would launch a study that would help to motivate most of the major educational initiatives of the past twenty years. The man who was primarily responsible was Terrel Bell, who President Reagan had appointed as the Secretary of Education. It was Bell who appointed the National Commission on Excellence, which would write the report known as *A Nation at Risk*. The *Biographical Dictionary of Modern American Educators* begins its biography of Secretary Bell with the assertion that he was "recruited by President Reagan to dismantle the United States Department of Education."[10] Needless to say, this did not happen, and Bell would have a busy and active tenure in the position until his resignation in 1985.

Terrel Bell was well qualified for the position of Secretary of Education. After receiving his bachelor's degree from Southern Idaho College, he served in the Marine Corps. Following his discharge, he worked as a science teacher and coach in Idaho. After earning a master's degree, he went on to act as a superintendent of schools in districts located in Idaho, Wyoming, and Utah. After completing his EdD. at the University of Utah, he was named Superintendent of Instruction for the state of Utah. He moved to Washington D.C. in 1970 to become Associate Commissioner of Education in the Department of Health, Education, and Welfare. During his tenure there, he had the opportunity to function as the acting Commissioner of Education. He left this position to serve again as a school superintendent but returned to the Education Department during the presidency of Gerald Ford.[11]

There was reason to question the value of an appointment as Ronald Reagan's Secretary of Education. The attitude of the leadership in the administration toward the Department of Education can be seen by a comment of Edwin Meese, the Attorney General and a close confidant of the president, who described the department as a "great bureaucratic joke."[12] The choice of Bell was somewhat surprising given the makeup of the rest of the cabinet. As a member of what some journalists referred to as the "millionaire's cabinet," Bell, a former school superintendent and professor, was something of an oddity, and he "was regularly badgered by administrative conservatives."[13] Bell, after leaving Washington D.C., reported that during his first month, he was "being nudged by the keepers of the conservative dogma" to close his office "and get out of town." Having rented a U-Haul to move to Washington D.C., he was asked whether he would "need some help with moving expenses" when he left town for Utah.[14]

As an administrator, the new secretary was faced with frustration when he attempted to fill leadership positions in his department. As part of the process, he was forced to accept conservatives who were pledged to help abolish the department. Edward Curran, who was given by the administration the position of director of the National Institute of Education, sent his recommendations directly to the president without even sharing a copy with his boss, the Secretary of Education. When Secretary Bell did offer a reorganization proposal, the funding was so minimal that it reduced the department to little more than a "financial-aid foundation."[15] Despite the fact that he was in a struggle for survival, Bell moved forward in 1981 to appoint a commission to make comprehensive recommendations on how to improve education in America. When the report *A Nation at Risk* was made public by the Commission in 1983, the president and his advisors saw it as a political opportunity in the 1984 campaign. Although the president endorsed the report, he chose to highlight his own priorities. The recommendations contained in the report did suggest that the responsibility for financing public education should remain with the state and local governments but it also said that the federal government "should help meet the needs of key groups of students such as the gifted and talented, the socioeconomically disadvantaged, minority and language-minority students, and the handicapped." Ignoring this part of the report, the president called for "an end to federal intrusion."[16]

Given the favorable public reception of the report, the President went on to make education a key element in his campaign for reelection in 1984. On sixty-two occasions during the campaign, he selectively quoted the report and at one point said publicly that he supported it "in its entirety." Encouraged, Secretary Bell worked enthusiastically for the president's reelection, but before Election Day he became aware that he had been "double-crossed." The Reagan administration, even during the campaign, was holding back funds that had already been approved for department programs. As it became clear to Secretary Bell that the administration had not really accepted the idea that the federal government would become an active participant in educational reform, he tendered his resignation on November 8, 1984. It was received with complete silence by the White House. Three days later, President Reagan told the press that Secretary Bell had resigned "for personal reasons." In December, Reagan said he would "hold up the appointment of a new Secretary of Education because we've never given up the belief that the department should be eliminated."[17]

Despite the lack of interest by the administration, the *Nation at Risk* report was instrumental in causing leaders at the state and local levels to seek solutions to the problems highlighted in the report. In order to understand these changes, it is necessary first to examine the makeup of the Commission and the work they did that led to their conclusions.

NOTES

1. Lou Cannon, *Reagan* (New York: Putnam, 1982), 109.

2. Harold Evans, *The American Century* (New York: Alfred A. Knopf, 1998), 612.

3. Edmund Morris, *Dutch: A Memoir of Ronald Reagan* (New York: Random House, 1999), 409.

4. Time-Life Books, *Pride and Prosperity: The 80s* (Alexandria, VA: Time-Life Books, 1999), 24–26.

5. Cannon, *Reagan*, 109.

6. Diane Ravitch, *Left Back: A Century of Battles over School Reform* (New York: Touchstone, 2000), 408.

7. Jack J. Nelson, Stuart B. Palonsky, and Mary Rose McCarthy, *Critical Issues in Education: Dialogues and Dialectics* (Boston: McGraw-Hill, 2004), 235.

8. Nelson, Palonsky, and McCarthy, *Critical Issues in Education*, 235.

9. Nelson, Palonsky, and McCarthy, *Critical Issues in Education*, 244.

10. Fredrick Ohles, Shirley Ohles, and John G. Ramsy, *Biographical Dictionary of Modern American Educators* (Westport, CT: Greenwood Press, 1997), 23.

11. Ohles, Ohles, and Ramsy, *Biographical Dictionary*, 23–24.

12. Cannon, *Reagan*, 86.

13. Cannon, *Reagan*, 813.

14. Wilbur Edel, *The Reagan Presidency: An Actor's Finest Performance* (New York: Hippocrene Books, 2000), 131.

15. Edel, *The Reagan Presidency*, 131.

16. Edel, *The Reagan Presidency*, 132.

17. Edel, *The Reagan Presidency*, 134.

CHAPTER 2

The Commission

When Terrel Bell began his tenure as the Secretary of Education, he was convinced that there were serious problems in our schools. As he considered what he could do in his new office to positively affect the status quo, he concluded that a report prepared by a group of respected individuals would be of interest and would be well received in the current climate. Some members of the Reagan administration attempted to discourage such a project on the grounds that task forces were often an excuse for not taking action. Looking back at history, Bell was convinced that there had been a number of such reports that had significant impact. He thought specifically of the Flexner study on medical education in 1910 and also about the report that led to the Marshall Plan to help rebuild Europe at the end of World War II. His initial idea was to have the president himself appoint a commission to study education in the United States. When he broached the proposal with those around the president he was rebuffed. Not only did some of President Reagan's advisors doubt the value of such a study, but they wished to avoid a major initiative by a department that the party platform had stated should be abolished.[1]

Because Bell continued to feel that it would be helpful to attempt to produce a report that would motivate our society to improve its educational system, he decided to go forward on his own initiative. It was his hope that he could establish a commission to produce a document that would hopefully shake the educational establishment in the same way as the launching of Sputnik had done during the 1950s. After learning the proper procedure, he decided to appoint a commission that would report directly to the Secretary of Education. Even in this effort his staff faced bureaucratic roadblocks and harassment. Some members of the administration even suggested that Secretary Bell was being insubordinate in establishing his own panel after it had been determined that the president would not appoint such a commission. Finally, in August 1981, a charter establishing the National Commission on Excellence in Education was completed. The next step was to appoint the members of the Commission. Prior to the appointments, conservatives within the presidential circle sought to ensure that the group be made up of those who agreed with Republican thinking on education. Bell, on the other hand, wished to appoint a balanced group.[2]

His first thought was to find a chairman who had the leadership skills and personal integrity to head a group with different backgrounds and who represented the major constituencies in the field of education. His choice for this important position was his friend David Gardner, who at that time was serving as the president of the University of Utah. During his eighteen months of leading the Commission, he was appointed president of the University of California. Bell chose as the Commission's senior staff associate, Dr. Milton Goldberg, a seasoned professional bureaucrat. It was Goldberg and his staff who were responsible for collecting, tabulating, and reporting the massive amounts of data gathered by the Commission. Because those who were appointed to the Commission held their own full-time jobs, the work of Goldberg and his assistants would be very important in framing the final conclusions and recommendations. For his part, Secretary Bell attempted to ensure that the Commission was given the financial support necessary to do its work. At the same time, he claims in his memoirs that he never attempted to influence the decisions of the group.[3]

The other members appointed to the National Commission on Excellence were as follows:

Yvonne W. Larson (Vice-Chair)	William O. Baker
Immediate Past-President	Chairman of the Board (Retired)
San Diego City School Board	Bell Telephone Laboratories
San Diego, California	Murray Hill, New Jersey

Anne Campbel
Former Commissioner of
    Education
State of Nebraska
Lincoln, Nebraska

Emeral A. Crosby
Principal
Northern High School
Detroit, Michigan

Charles A. Foster Jr.
Immediate Past-President
Foundation for Teaching
    Economics
San Francisco, California

Norman C. Francis
President
Xavier University of
    Louisiana
New Orleans, Louisianaa

A. Bartlett Giamatti
President
Yale University
New Haven, Connecticut

Shirley Gordon
President
Highline Community College
Midway, Washington

Roberts V. Haderlein
Immediate Past-President
National School Boards
    Association
Girard, Kansas

Gerald Holton
Mallinckrodt Professor of
    Physics and
Professor of the History of
    Science
Harvard University
Cambridge, Massachusetts

Annette Y. Kirk
Kirk Associates
Mecosta, Michigan

Margaret S. Marston
Member
Virginia State Board of
    Education
Arlington, Virginia

Albert H. Quie
Former Governor
State of Minnesota
St. Paul, Minnesota

Francisco D. Sanchez Jr.
Superintendent of Schools
Albuquerque Public Schools
Albuquerque, New Mexico

Glenn T. Seaborg
University Professor of
    Chemistry and Nobel
    Laureate
University of California
Berkeley, California

Jay Sommer   Richard Wallace
National Teacher of the Year,   Principal
   1981–1982   Lutheran High School East
Foreign Language Department   Cleveland Heights, Ohio[4]
New Rochelle High School
New Rochelle, New York

In making his appointments, Secretary Bell attempted to include a very diverse group of individuals. Dr. William Baker was a distinguished scientist, while Bartlett Giamatti was serving as a college president. Giamatti later became well known as the Commissioner of Baseball. Dr. Norman Francis was a black scholar who also served as a college president. The Hispanic community was represented by Dr. Francisco Sanchez, a superintendent of schools. The governor of Minnesota and the 1981 Teacher of the Year were also panel members, along with both a public and a private school principal. School boards also had a spokesman in the person of Robert Haderlein. The group was given eighteen months to study the problems of education and to make a final report in March of 1983.[5]

Secretary Bell furnished the Commission with a mission statement in which he outlined the purpose and functions of the group. They were as follows:

1. To review and synthesize the data and scholarly literature on the quality of learning and teaching in the nation's schools, colleges, and universities, both public and private, with special concern for educational experience of teenage youth;

2. To examine and to compare and contrast the curricula, standards, and expectations of the educational systems of several advanced countries with those of the United States;

3. To study a representative sampling of university and college admission standards and lower division course requirements with particular reference to the impact upon the enhancement of quality and the promotion of excellence such standards may have on high school curricula and on expected levels of high school academic achievement;

4. To review and to describe educational programs that are recognized as preparing students who consistently attain higher than average scores in college entrance examinations and who meet

with uncommon success the demands placed on them by the nation's colleges and universities;

5. To review the major changes that have occurred in American education as well as events in society during the past quarter century that have significantly affected educational achievement;

6. To hold hearings and to receive testimony and expert advice on efforts that could and should be taken to foster higher levels of quality and academic excellence in the nation's schools, colleges, and universities;

7. To do all other things needed to define the problems of and the barriers to attaining greater levels of excellence in American education; and

8. To report and to make practical recommendations for action to be taken by educators, public officials, governing boards, parents, and others having a vital interest in American education and a capacity to influence it for the better.[6]

To carry out these tasks the Commission was assigned a budget of $785,000. As part of the budget, Commission members were to be paid one hundred dollars per day plus expenses. The budget line for staff allowed for up to sixteen positions. Notice of all meetings was to be published, and meetings were to be held in public unless a private meeting was approved by the Assistant Secretary for Educational Research and Improvement.[7]

Along with the eight general meetings of the Commission members, the staff gained input from "educators, students, professional and public groups, parents, public officials and scholars; existing analyses of problems in education; letters from concerned citizens, teachers, and administrators; and descriptions of notable programs and promising approaches on education."[8]

The public events of the Commission began with a meeting on October 9 and 10, 1981. The final session did not occur until June 23, 1983. Five of the sessions, which were held in five different states, addressed specific topics. The subjects discussed give a clue as to the Commission's research priorities. The list of topics is included below:

1. Mathematics and Technology Education
2. Language and Literacy: Skills for Academic Learning

3. Performance Expectations in American Education
4. Teaching and Teacher Education
5. College Admissions and the Transition to Postsecondary Education[9]

Along with the testimony given at these meetings, there were twenty other authorities who made presentations to the Commission. These presentations included reports from college professors, state education officials, and representatives of business.[10]

There were also twenty-six commissioned papers that were prepared to provide additional research. Among these publications were works such as "An Analytic Comparison of Educational Systems" and "What Is Learned in Schools: Responding to School Demands, K–6."[11] In addition, "over two hundred schools, school districts, colleges, and other educational organizations" submitted descriptions of what the report labels as "Notable Programs." These too were used in developing the final recommendations of the Commission.

Once the data was gathered, the staff prepared summaries and began to study possible solutions for the problems identified. The solutions would be considered by the Commission members who would seek to agree on recommendations to deal with each of the problem areas. It was the goal of Chairman Gardner to reach a consensus on all aspects of the final report. This proved to be very difficult, and as a result the group asked for and was granted an extension on the deadline given to complete its work. Secretary Bell had arranged time on the president's schedule for releasing the report, but because it was unfinished a new date for the release had to be secured. Although some of the staff members doubted that the group would reach a consensus, Gardner continued to press the members to agree on the final draft. Until the end, it was feared that several members would file minority reports and that this type of division would only weaken the impact of the Commission's work.[12]

The unanimity achieved by the Commission is quite obvious in the Letter of Transmittal that accompanied the report. This letter is printed below:

April 26, 1983
Honorable T.H. Bell
Secretary of Education
U.S. Department of Education
Washington, D.C. 20202

Dear Mr. Secretary:

On August 26, 1981, you created the National Commission on Excellence in Education and directed it to present a report on the quality of education in America to you and to the American people by April of 1983.

It has been my privilege to chair this endeavor and on behalf of the members of the Commission it is my pleasure to transmit this report, *A Nation at Risk: The Imperative for Educational Reform.*

Our purpose has been to help define the problems afflicting American education and to provide solutions, not search for scapegoats. We addressed the main issues as we saw them, but have not attempted to treat the subordinate matters in any detail. We were forthright in our discussions and have been candid in our report regarding both the strengths and weaknesses of American education.

The Commission deeply believes that the problems we have discerned in American education can be both understood and corrected if the people of our country, together with those who have public responsibility in the matter, care enough and are courageous enough to do what is required.

Each member of the Commission appreciates your leadership in having asked this diverse group of persons to examine one of the central issues which will define our Nation's future. We especially welcomed your confidence throughout the course of our deliberations and your anticipation of a report free of political partisanship.

It is our collective and earnest hope that you will continue to provide leadership in this effort by assuring wide dissemination and full discussion of this report, and by encouraging appropriate action throughout the country. We believe that materials compiled by the Commission in the course of its work constitute a major resource for all persons interested in American education.

The other Commissioners and I sincerely appreciate the opportunity to have served our country as members of the National Commission on Education, and on their behalf I remain,

Respectfully,

David Pierpont Gardner
Chairman

As the day approached for the release of the report, there was a conflict within the administration concerning the president's speech during the ceremony. The conservatives led by Attorney General Meese wanted the president to use the occasion to highlight the Republican position on issues such as school prayer, tuition tax credits for private schools, and the evils of the National Education Association. None of these topics were considered in the report, and therefore Secretary Bell thought that they would be inappropriate subjects for the ceremony releasing the report. Although the conservatives were successful in including several of the issues in the president's remarks, they were not picked up in the extensive press and media coverage that followed the meeting. The response to the report far exceeded anything that those who had prepared it could have expected. It was on the front page of every major newspaper and was actually published in its entirety in some newspapers. Editorials of support also appeared in many newspapers and periodicals. Evening news programs on all three of the major networks featured stories on the report. Both Chairman Gardner and Secretary Bell quickly received numerous speaking invitations. In a matter of days, the condition of our educational system in the nation became a major issue in the media.[13]

After this very positive initial reaction, Secretary Bell followed up with a series of dissemination conferences held at locations throughout the country. President Reagan chose to appear at a number of these meetings to underscore his commitment to the report and to improving our schools. Another initiative taken by the Department of Education that would be of major importance in bringing about change was a project that would allow the department to compare student achievement among the states. This gave governors data they had not had before. Especially for those states whose students were not doing well, the test scores provided immediate motivation for change. Perhaps the single most successful event in implementing the recommendations of the report occurred when Secretary Bell had the opportunity to meet with all of the governors while they were visiting Vice President Bush in the state of Maine. At this meeting, Secretary Bell was able to impress upon the executives of all the states the fact that our schools were not performing as well as they might.[14]

It would be the governors who would carry the message of the need for reform back to their home states. Many of these state leaders worked quickly to develop proposals to submit to their legislatures and state boards of education. In a relatively short span of time, changes were occurring in numerous states. The authors of various education textbooks have concluded that the impact of the *A Nation at Risk* report, along with a number of other similar reports, was a primary factor in the reform movements that have taken place in education during the past two decades. For example, the sixth edition of a popular teacher education text, *Teachers, Schools, and Society*, listed six major initiatives that occurred during the first two years after the *A Nation at Risk* report was published:

- Hundreds of local state panels were formed.
- More than forty states increased course requirements for graduation.
- Thirty-three states instituted testing for student promotion or graduation.
- Almost half the states passed legislation to increase qualification standards and pay for teachers.
- Most states increased the length of the school day and/or school year.
- Most states passed laws that required teachers and students to demonstrate computer literacy.[15]

In order to understand the impact of the report, it would undoubtedly be helpful to provide a summary of the major ideas contained in the *A Nation at Risk* report. This summary is the purpose of the next chapter.

NOTES

1. Terrel H. Bell, *The Thirteenth Man* (New York: The Free Press, 1988), 114–15.
2. Bell, *The Thirteenth Man*, 116–17.
3. Bell, *The Thirteenth Man*, 116–17.
4. U.S. Department of Education, The National Commission on Excellence in Education, *A Nation at Risk: The Imperative for Educational Reform*, April 1983, 1–2.
5. Bell, *The Thirteenth Man*, 117–18.
6. U.S. Department of Education, *A Nation at Risk*, app. A, 1–2.
7. U.S. Department of Education, *A Nation at Risk*, app. A, 2.

8. Beatrice Gross and Ronald Gross, eds., *The School Debate* (New York: Simon & Schuster, 1985), 55.

9. U.S. Department of Education, *A Nation at Risk*, app. B, 1–2.

10. U.S. Department of Education, *A Nation at Risk*, app. E, 1.

11. U.S. Department of Education, *A Nation at Risk*, app. C, 1–2.

12. Bell, *The Thirteenth Man*, 120–25.

13. Bell, *The Thirteenth Man*, 28–32.

14. Bell, *The Thirteenth Man*, 135.

15. Myra Pollack Sadker and David Miller Sadker, *Teachers, Schools, and Society* (McGraw-Hill, 2003), 149.

CHAPTER 3

The Report

Rather than including the text in its entirety, it would seem sufficient for the purposes of this book to summarize the highlights of the Commission's report. In the introduction, in the paragraphs following the often-quoted second paragraph (see preface, page viii), the authors begin with a statement that as a nation we have "lost sight of the basic purpose of schooling." In several sections in the report, the importance of reading, math, and science is mentioned. For most readers who consider the total text, it is difficult to escape the conclusion that this is a plea for schools to go "back to basics." This is true even though the authors concede that

> some worry that schools may emphasize such rudiments as reading and computation at the expense of other essential skills such as comprehension, analysis, solving problems, and drawing conclusions. Still others are concerned that an overemphasis on technical and occupational skills will leave little time for studying the arts and humanities that so enrich daily life, help maintain civility, and develop a sense of community. Knowledge of the humanities, they maintain, must be harnessed to science and technology if the latter are to remain creative and humane, just as the humanities need to be informed by science and technology if they are to remain relevant to the human condition.[1]

Despite its strong criticism of schools, the Commission does not place the primary blame on teachers and administrators. Instead, it suggests that the decline has been caused by unreasonable and unattainable demands on schools to solve "personal, social, and political problems that the home and other institutions either will not or cannot resolve."[2]

Later in the text the authors express their serious concern over the proliferation of electives in our high schools. These new courses were often offered in response to pressure from communities or from the state governments.

Throughout the introductory portion of the report, a primary theme is the loss of our nation's "preeminence in commerce, industry, science, and technological innovation."[3] These competitive losses to other nations appeared to be the most significant reason that we are considered at risk as a nation. The text actually mentions our failure to compete effectively with Japan, Germany, and South Korea and points directly to a "rising tide of mediocrity" in our schools, which threatens our future as a nation. According to the analysis, we are part of a "global village," and we can no longer depend on our rich natural resources to ensure our edge over our "determined, well-educated, and strongly motivated competition."[4] Although the need to improve our competitive position in the world is an important goal of the report, it is not the only reason given for improving our nation's educational program.

The authors also mention the need to foster in our schools the "intellectual, moral, and spiritual strengths of our people." In justifying this function of schools, the report emphasizes the need to prepare our students to become active citizens. This plea is enforced by including this quotation of Thomas Jefferson:

> I know no safe depository of the ultimate powers but the people themselves; and if we think them not enlightened enough to exercise their control with a wholesome discretion, the remedy is not to take from them but to inform their discretion.[5]

This introductory section of the report closes with a discussion of the responsibilities of society to provide an excellent education to "all children" whatever their race, gender, or economic class. To prove that our schools are not meeting these challenges, the text includes a list of statistics labeled "Indicators of the Risk." A number of these factors are listed below.

- International comparisons of student achievement, completed a decade ago, reveal that on nineteen academic tests American students were never first or second and, in comparison with other industrialized nations, were last seven times.

- Some 23 million American adults are functionally illiterate by the simplest tests of everyday reading, writing, and comprehension.
- About 13 percent of all seventeen-year-olds in the United States can be considered functionally illiterate.
- Average achievement of high school students on most standardized tests is now lower than twenty-six years ago when Sputnik was launched.
- The College Board's Scholastic Aptitude Tests (SAT) demonstrate virtually unbroken decline from 1963 to 1980. Average verbal scores fell over fifty points, and average mathematics scores dropped nearly forty points.
- There was a steady decline in science achievement scores of U.S seventeen-year-olds as measured by national assessments of science in 1969, 1973, and 1977.
- Average tested achievement of students graduating from college is also lower.
- Business and military leaders complain that they are required to spend millions of dollars on costly remedial education and training programs in such basic skills as reading, writing, spelling, and computation. The Department of the Navy, for example, reported to the Commission that one-quarter of its recent recruits cannot read at the ninth grade level, the minimum needed simply to understand written safety instructions.[6]

Following this list, the report goes on to highlight our failures in science education. The authors quote two authorities who are critical of what schools are doing in this area. The first statement is from education researcher Paul Hurd who concluded after a national survey on student achievement in science that "we are raising a new generation of Americans that is scientifically and technologically illiterate." Another aspect of the problem is noted by John Slaughter who had served as the Director of the National Science Foundation. He is quoted as saying that we have "a growing chasm between a small scientific and technological elite and a citizenry ill-informed, indeed uninformed, on issues with a science component."[7]

The section dealing with Indicators of the Risk ends with the assertion that our current graduates of schools and colleges are less well educated than the graduates twenty-five or thirty-five years ago.[8] This claim we will find is one that is widely disputed by many of the critics of the report.

The next major heading of the report is entitled "Hope and Frustration." Here it is argued that Americans are unhappy and frustrated with the "shoddiness" in many areas of American life, including our schools. Again in this section, the report refers to the shrinking job market with the implication that some of the downturn in our economy is related to our poor educational system. Even though the authors point to a high degree of dissatisfaction with our schools, they do caution against the futility of seeking "scapegoats" such as our teachers.

The hopeful signs noted include the apparent national consensus concerning the need to improve math and science education. Other subjects mentioned in this section include English, history, geography, economics, and foreign language. It would appear from this and other sections of the report that the primary goal for reforming our schools would be to put additional emphasis on these classes that the Commission feels are basic to an excellent academic education.

The next section of the Introduction deals with the topic "Excellence in Education." For the authors, excellence means "several related things." These include high expectations for all students rather than the "minimum standards" adopted by a number of states. It is in this portion of the report that we first read about the need for "standards," a word and concept that would spread throughout the country during the next two decades. There is also the thought expressed that we must raise our expectations for students to allow them "to work to the limits of their capabilities."[9]

A section defining "The Learning Society" occurs next in the report. The emphasis in this paragraph is that learning must be seen as a life-long activity for all of our citizens. Competition and rapid change, it is suggested, will not allow us to be complacent if we are not to have our knowledge and skills become rapidly outdated. The importance of schools in this scheme of the Learning Society is expressed this way: "In our view, formal schooling in youth is the essential foundation for learning throughout one's life." Again a criticism is included of the practice of schools to accept "minimum requirements," and a plea is made for a "coherent continuum of learning." At the end of this portion of the report, the Commission discusses the need for all groups in our society—including parents, students, teachers, administrators, school board members, colleges, businesses, union members, military leaders, governors, state legislators, the president, members of Congress and other public officials, members of the learned and scientific societies, representatives of the print and electronic media, and concerned citizens everywhere—to work together because "America is at risk."[10]

It is important to know that the Commission's views are not just expressed as "doom and gloom." The introductory portion of the report goes on to argue that we have the "Tools at Hand" to solve our educational problems. In making this point, the authors list a number of positive factors that will make change possible. Several of the most prominent advantages are listed below:

- The natural abilities of the young that cry out to be developed and the undiminished concern of the parents for the well-being of their children;
- The persistent and authentic American dream that superior performance can raise one's state in life and shape one's own future;
- The dedication, against all odds, that keeps teachers serving in schools and colleges, even as the rewards diminish;
- Our better understanding of learning and teaching and the implications of this knowledge for school practice, and the numerous examples of local success as a result of superior effort and effective dissemination;
- The equally sound tradition, from the Northwest Ordinance of 1787 until today, that the federal government should supplement state, local, and other resources to foster key national educational goals.[11]

It should be noted that the last item on this list is again the claim that the federal government should be a partner in the effort to provide true excellence in our nation's schools.

The final subsection in the Introduction states that the public is ready to support efforts to improve our schools. This point of view is illustrated by citing public opinion polls that place education as the "top priority" in solving the problems facing the United States. Also mentioned is the strong public support for more demanding academic standards. Finally, in the last two sentences of the Introduction, the authors return to the theme of economics:

The citizen is dismayed at a steady 15-year decline in industrial productivity, as one great American industry after another falls to world competition. The citizen wants the country to act on the belief, expressed in our hearings and by the large majority in the Gallup Poll, that education should be at the top of the Nation's agenda.[12]

After the Introduction, the next major part of the report is entitled "Findings." Here the authors have divided the data that has been collected into four subheadings. Under each of these titles is a group of statements that summarize the results of the research done by the Commission and its staff. The first of these sections is called "Findings Regarding Content." The results of the research dealing with content include comparisons of high school course patterns in the period 1964 to 1969 with those classes offered between 1976 and 1981. Based on this research, the Commission concluded that secondary school curriculum had been "homogenized, diluted, and diffused." The report noted that only 31 percent of current graduates had completed intermediate algebra, 13 percent French I, 16 percent geography, and 6 percent calculus. They also criticized the growth of the number of "general track students" who were devoting 25 percent of their credits to classes such as physical education, work experience, remedial English and math, as well as courses preparing students for adulthood and marriage.[13]

The second part of this section deals with expectations for students. These expectations are expressed in several different ways:

- By grades, which reflect the degree to which students demonstrate their mastery of subject matter
- Through high school and college graduation requirements, which tell students which subjects are most important
- By the presence or absence of rigorous examinations requiring students to demonstrate their mastery of content and skill before receiving a diploma or a degree
- By college admissions requirements, which reinforce high school standards
- By the difficulty of the subject matter students confront in their texts and assigned readings

Based on these factors the Commission then included a number of "notable deficiencies." There are ten of these problem areas listed. Because these findings are the basis for many of the recommendations to follow, it is helpful to include the entire list below:

- The amount of homework for high school seniors has decreased (two-thirds report less than one hour a night) and grades have risen as average student achievement has been declining.
- In many other industrialized nations, courses in mathematics (other than arithmetic or general mathematics), biology, chemistry, physics, and geography start in grade 6 and are required of all students. The time spent on these subjects, based on class hours, is about three times that spent by even the most science-oriented U.S. students, i.e., those who select four years of science and mathematics in secondary school.
- A 1980 state-by-state survey of high school diploma requirements reveals that only eight states require high schools to offer foreign language instruction, but none require students to take the courses. Thirty-five states require only one year of mathematics, and thirty-six require only one year of science for a diploma.
- In thirteen states, 50 percent or more of the units required for high school graduation may be electives chosen by the student. Given this freedom to choose the substance of half or more of their education, many students opt for less demanding personal service courses, such as bachelor living.
- "Minimum competency" examinations (now required in thirty-seven states) fall short of what is needed, as the "minimum" tends to become the "maximum," thus lowering educational standards for all.
- One-fifth of all four-year public colleges in the United States must accept every high school graduate within the state regardless of program followed or grades, thereby serving notice to high school students that they can expect to attend college even if they do not follow a demanding course of study in high school or perform well.
- About 23 percent of our more selective colleges and universities reported that their general level of selectivity declined during the 1970s, and 29 percent reported reducing the number of specific high school courses required for admission (usually by dropping foreign language requirements, which are now specified as a condition for admission by only one-fifth of our institutions of higher education).

- Too few experienced teachers and scholars are involved in writing textbooks. During the past decade or so a large number of texts have been "written down" by their publishers to ever-lower reading levels in response to perceived market demands.
- A recent study by Education Products Information Exchange revealed that a majority of students were able to master 80 percent of the material in some their subject-matter texts before they had even opened the books. Many books do not challenge the students to whom they are assigned.
- Expenditures for textbooks and other instructional materials have declined by 50 percent over the past seventeen years. While some recommend a level of spending on texts of between 5 and 10 percent of the operating costs of schools, the budgets for basal texts and related materials have been dropping during the past decade and a half to only 0.7 percent today.[14]

In the third portion of this section, the Commission shares its concern about the lack of time available for instruction in our schools. It cites the fact that in England it is not unusual for students to be in school eight hours a day for 220 days while their counterparts in the United States are in school for six hours a day for 180 days. Pointing to courses like driver education and home economics, the implication of the authors is that these classes are also using valuable instructional time that could be used to teach basic subjects. Another problem in American schools is illustrated by a California study reporting that "poor classroom management was wasting twenty percent of the time allotted for teaching reading comprehension." Finally, this section expressed the opinion that our students could increase their academic success if they had adequate study skills.[15]

The last subject addressed in the Findings section of the report dealt with teaching. Here it was claimed that the profession was not attracting the best and brightest of the high school graduates. Teacher-training programs also come under fire for overemphasizing "educational methods courses" and failing to include sufficient content area preparation. One survey noted that 41 percent of the time of a student's preparation to become an elementary teacher was being spent in education classes. At the same time the authors were critical of teacher education, they also lamented poor teacher salaries. The report said that the average annual salary of a teacher after twelve years of experience was only $18,000. Critical shortages of qualified teachers were noted in such fields as "mathematics, science, and foreign languages; and among specialists in education for the gifted and talented, language minority and handicapped students." The lack of mathematics and physics teachers was specifically pointed out. Especially alarming was the statistic that one-half of the newly appointed teachers in mathematics were not qualified to teach the subject. Finally, the lack of teacher participation in areas such as textbook selection was noted.[16]

In the next major section, the Commission gives its recommendations in each of the problem areas highlighted in the Findings section of the report. At the outset it is made clear that these recommendations deal with both public and private schools as well as colleges.

In the area of content, the report recommends a high school curriculum that includes

- Four years of English
- Three years of mathematics
- Three years of science
- Three years of social studies
- One-half year of computer science
- Two years of foreign language in high school are strongly recommended in addition to those taken earlier.[17]

This curriculum is labeled the "New Basics." It should be noted that, along with English, social studies, math, and science, the fifth course considered basic by the authors is computer education. In 1983 when this report was released, many schools throughout the country were requiring only one class in math and science for those students not planning to attend college. During the same period only a few students were taking foreign language, and computer classes were rare. In what some saw as an afterthought, there was mention of "work in the fine and performing arts," but these subjects were not labeled as part of the "New Basics."

Following the list of proposed requirements, the authors further defined what would be the basis for the courses in each required curriculum area. The ideas included were undoubtedly considered when curriculum standards were later written by state and federal officials. For instance, in explaining what should be expected in science classes, the report suggests that "the teaching of science in high school should provide graduates with an introduction to:

- The concepts, laws, and processes of the physical and biological sciences
- The methods of scientific inquiry and reasoning
- The application of scientific knowledge to everyday life
- The social and environmental implications of scientific and technological development."

A second example would be in the area of social studies, which the report stated should be designed to:

- Enable students to fix their places and possibilities within the larger social and cultural structure
- Understand the broad sweep of both ancient and contemporary ideas that have shaped our world
- Understand the fundamentals of how our economic system works and how our political system functions
- Grasp the difference between free and repressive societies[18]

With the study of foreign language the Commission suggested that "proficiency in a foreign language requires from four to six years of study." As a result, they urged that it should be started in the elementary school.[19] Needless to say, in 1983 only a few school districts were beginning a foreign language before high school. Even though foreign language study was mentioned several times in the report, it was not considered one of the "New Basics." The report also calls for the need to raise the academic expectations for students in vocational classes. In grades one through eight, the authors merely ask that the curriculum should build a solid base "in such areas as English, language development and writing, computational and problem-solving skills, science, social studies, foreign language, and the arts."[20]

Related to the finding dealing with "Standards and Expectations," the following recommendation was highlighted:

We recommend that schools, colleges, and universities adopt more rigorous and measurable standards, and higher expectations, for academic performance and student conduct, and that 4-year colleges and universities raise their requirements for admission. This will help students do their best educationally with challenging materials in an environment that supports learning and authentic accomplishment.[21]

The key ideas in this recommendation are the words "rigorous" and "measurable." Not only were they telling schools that they should be demanding more of students but that these more rigorous standards must be measurable. In most states, measurements meant examinations. The implied message was that schools must be more accountable in the areas of student achievement. In almost every case, the preferred method of determining the level of accountability has become "high-stakes testing." There is no question that the introduction of new examinations at every level has become one of the most important and controversial reforms that began in the decade of the 80s.[22]

In implementing this recommendation, the Commission proposed the following objectives. Grades for students "should be indicative of academic achievement so they can be relied on as evidence of a student's readiness for further study."[23] This comment implies that many schools may be guilty of what has become know as "grade inflation." The report also refers to the need for colleges and universities to raise their admission requirements by instituting standardized achievement tests in the five basic areas of the curriculum, "and where applicable, foreign languages." The report is also critical of using standardized aptitude tests rather than those that measure academic achievement. Although it is suggested that tests be administered nationwide, the authors fall short of suggesting a national testing system. The proposed state and local tests should be used not only to evaluate students' progress but for diagnostic purposes.[24]

In the effort to raise standards, the authors recommend that textbooks be upgraded and updated in order to provide students with more challenging content. Funds should be made available to encourage publishers to prepare textbooks in "thin-market" areas such as special education and classes for gifted and talented students. Other companies should be encouraged to develop learning materials utilizing technology in every curriculum area.[25]

The report goes on to include a number of suggestions for allowing students more time for academics. These include ways to make "more effective use of the existing school day, a longer school day, or a lengthened school year." Along with increasing the time students spend in school, the Commission suggests that high school students be given more homework. In order to make better use of their time, students should be instructed in "effective study and work skills." The report goes as far as to suggest that school districts and state legislatures "strongly consider seven-hour school days, as well as a 200–220-day school year." In addition, it is recommended that schools work to improve classroom management by developing "firm and fair codes of student conduct that are enforced consistently, and by considering alternative classrooms, programs, and schools to meet the needs of continually disruptive students." To improve attendance, the suggestion is to provide clear incentives and sanctions to ensure that students are in attendance and on time. The report indirectly criticizes the practice known as "social promotion," by recommending that promotion to the next grade level and the awarding of a diploma be based on "the academic progress of students and their instructional needs, rather than by rigid adherence to age."[26]

In the area of teaching, the Commission agreed on a series of recommendations aimed at making teaching "a more rewarding and respected profession." The first suggestion was that colleges and universities preparing teachers should be required to maintain high standards for teacher candidates. At the secondary level, these teachers should be required to demonstrate "competence in their academic discipline." School districts should be offering their teachers higher salaries, but teachers should expect that salaries would be "performance based." An effective teacher evaluation system should be in place in all school districts, and it should include "peer review so that superior teachers can be rewarded, average ones encouraged, and poor ones either improved or terminated." In order to give teachers more time to plan, teachers could be given an eleven-month contract to prepare curriculum, participate in professional development, and work with students with special needs. "Career ladders" should be created that would distinguish between "the beginning instructor, the experienced teacher, and the master teacher." The report also urges that, especially in academic areas in which there is a shortage of teachers, alternative programs should be established to prepare liberal arts graduates for positions in education. To induce outstanding college students into the field of education, grants and loans should be made available, especially in areas such as math and science.[27]

The last area in which recommendations are made is entitled "Leadership and Fiscal Support." What is suggested in this portion of the report is "that citizens across the Nation hold educators and elected officials responsible for providing the leadership necessary to achieve these reforms, and that citizens give the fiscal support and stability required to bring about the reforms we propose."[28] It is in this section that the concept of accountability is introduced. Most likely, it was the business representatives on the Commission who were especially interested in making schools more accountable for producing measurable academic progress with their students.

Traditionally, educators have been somewhat reluctant to attempt to quantify educational outcomes and to assign responsibility when expectations are not met. Many would argue that positive outcomes of an educational program cannot be determined solely by standardized tests. They also would point out that students attending our schools vary greatly in academic motivation and parental support. As a result, those working in an inner-city school where many students have a primary language other than English or have few educational advantages in their home, should not be expected to produce the same amount of educational growth as schools located in wealthy suburbs. Despite the argument, the report does not back away from assigning responsibility to "educators and elected officials." At the same time, the authors maintain that it is the job of society to provide adequate financial help whatever the educational challenges and to assist those in leadership positions in doing their job.[29]

This section of the document is clear in its description of the type of leadership that is necessary. It talks about a participatory approach that allows the building of a consensus among teachers, parents, and community members. Also mentioned is the leadership responsibility of school board members and state officials. The role assigned to the federal government would be primarily to provide assistance to students who are disadvantaged or have disabilities. It is pointed out that the federal bureaucracy should attempt to be unobtrusive and place a minimal amount of administrative burden on schools.[30]

Following the recommendation section of the report, the Commission adds some words of encouragement to those who are willing to accept the challenge of improving our schools. In three paragraphs found under the heading "America Can Do It," the authors review past accomplishments of our schools and colleges. The report highlights the fact that we graduate approximately 75 percent of our high school students and that the percentage of college age students enrolled in institutions of higher learning exceeds all of our economic rivals in the world. Despite the fact that our average test scores are lower than most Western nations, the top 9 percent of American students compare favorably with their peers in nations around the world. In this section it is also noted that achievement scores are improving in many of our larger urban areas and that our schools are doing a much better job in offering special programs for our gifted and talented students. In the words of the report, "we are the inheritors of a past that gives us every reason to believe that we will succeed."[31]

At the end of the recommendations portion of the text, the authors address both parents and students. They ask parents to help their children to develop strong character and a respect and desire for knowledge. Parents are urged to teach their children a positive work ethic, and they are reminded that they are their "child's first and most influential teacher." As a result, it is important that they "be a living example." In addition, parents are asked to "participate actively in their child's education" and to model in their own lives a commitment to continual learning. Also, parents should instill in their offspring the importance of "intellectual and moral integrity." Finally, both parents and teachers are once again reminded that children will look to them as their models for all of these virtues.[32]

Students are told that "you forfeit your chance for life at the fullest when you withhold your best effort in learning." They are reminded that although parents and teachers can encourage them, in the end it is their own effort and level of commitment that will make the difference. All students are urged to use their "gifts and talents" and to "work with dedication and self-discipline." If they will only maintain high expectations for themselves, they will be able to "convert every challenge into an opportunity."[33]

At the end of the Recommendations section of the document, the Commission offers a "Final Word." Here they point to the fact that

children born today can expect to graduate from high school in the year 2000. We dedicate our report not only to these children, but also to those now in school and others to come. We firmly believe that a movement of America's schools in the direction called for by our recommendations will prepare these children for far more effective lives in a far stronger America. . . . It is by our willingness to take up the challenge, and our resolve to see it through, that America's place in the world will be either secured or forfeited. Americans have succeeded before and so we shall again.[34]

Following the Recommendations, the report includes seven additional sections, which are listed below:

* Appendix A: Charter—National Commission on Excellence in Education
* Appendix B: Schedule of the Commission's Public Events
* Appendix C: Commissioned Papers
* Appendix D: Hearing Testimony
* Appendix E: Other Presentations to the Commission
* Appendix F: Notable Programs
* Appendix G: Acknowledgments

Readers wishing access to the entire report can find it at www.ed.gov/pubs/NatAtRisk/index.html.

Even though most historians are in agreement that this report was a significant event in the history of education in the United States, it would be a gross simplification of history to suggest that the numerous other reports and books published during the same time period did not influence the course of events in our schools. In order to understand the events and trends of the last two decades, it is necessary to consider the other major publications that have combined with *A Nation at Risk* to affect recent history.

NOTES

1. U.S. Department of Education, The National Commission on Excellence in Education, *A Nation at Risk: The Imperative for Educational Reform*, April 1983, Introduction, 4.
2. U.S. Department of Education, *A Nation at Risk*, Introduction, 1.
3. U.S. Department of Education, *A Nation at Risk*, Introduction, 1.
4. U.S. Department of Education, *A Nation at Risk*, Introduction, 2.

5. U.S. Department of Education, *A Nation at Risk*, Introduction, 2.

6. U.S. Department of Education, *A Nation at Risk*, Introduction, 2–3.

7. U.S. Department of Education, *A Nation at Risk*, Introduction, 2.

8. U.S. Department of Education, *A Nation at Risk*, Introduction, 4.

9. U.S. Department of Education, *A Nation at Risk*, Introduction, 4.

10. U.S. Department of Education, *A Nation at Risk*, Introduction, 5.

11. U.S. Department of Education, *A Nation at Risk*, Introduction, 6.

12. U.S. Department of Education, *A Nation at Risk*, Introduction, 7.

13. U.S. Department of Education, *A Nation at Risk*, Introduction, 8.

14. U.S. Department of Education, *A Nation at Risk*, Findings, 1–2.

15. U.S. Department of Education, *A Nation at Risk*, Findings, 2.

16. U.S. Department of Education, *A Nation at Risk*, Findings, 3.

17. U.S. Department of Education, *A Nation at Risk*, Recommendations, 1.

18. U.S. Department of Education, *A Nation at Risk*, Recommendations, 2.

19. U.S. Department of Education, *A Nation at Risk*, Recommendations, 2.

20. U.S. Department of Education, *A Nation at Risk*, Recommendations, 2.

21. U.S. Department of Education, *A Nation at Risk*, Recommendations, 3.

22. U.S. Department of Education, *A Nation at Risk*, Recommendations, 3.

23. U.S. Department of Education, *A Nation at Risk*, Recommendations, 3.

24. U.S. Department of Education, *A Nation at Risk*, Recommendations, 3.

25. U.S. Department of Education, *A Nation at Risk*, Recommendations, 3.

26. U.S. Department of Education, *A Nation at Risk*, Recommendations, 3–4.

27. U.S. Department of Education, *A Nation at Risk*, Recommendations, 4.

28. U.S. Department of Education, *A Nation at Risk*, Recommendations, 5.

29. U.S. Department of Education, *A Nation at Risk*, Leadership and Fiscal Support, 5.

30. U.S. Department of Education, *A Nation at Risk*, Leadership and Fiscal Support, 5.

31. U.S. Department of Education, *A Nation at Risk*, Leadership and Fiscal Support, 6.

32. U.S. Department of Education, *A Nation at Risk*, Leadership and Fiscal Support, 6–7.

33. U.S. Department of Education, *A Nation at Risk*, A Word to Parents and Students, 7.

34. U.S. Department of Education, *A Nation at Risk*, Leadership and Fiscal Support, 6–7.

CHAPTER 4

The Others

Even before the release of the *A Nation at Risk* report, philosopher Mortimer Adler published in 1982 a report calling for a "back to basics" approach to curriculum. Entitled the Paideia Proposal and written by twenty-two national, state, and local educators, the report was a philosophical defense of a liberal arts curriculum as the basis for the uniform education for all students in grades one through twelve. For Adler and his fellow authors, any variation from their liberal arts curriculum that included electives would be an "unconscionable deviation from the good." The only electives in this plan would be a choice of foreign language to study.[1]

This report goes on to argue that a true liberal arts curriculum can offer students "an exciting, involving, intellectual and aesthetic journey." The authors believe that such a curriculum could be made meaningful to all students, whether they be gifted children from wealthy suburban districts or minority children from an urban area. The book argues strongly against a differentiated curriculum because it is felt that all children need to be prepared for lifelong learning, and a basic liberal arts curriculum is the best way to accomplish this objective.[2] In Mortimer Adler's own words:

> In the first 80 years of this century, we have met the obligation imposed on us by the principle of equal educational opportunity, but only in a quantitative sense. Now, as we approach the end of the century, we must achieve equality in qualitative terms.
>
> This means a one-track system of schooling. It means, at the basic level, giving all the young the same kind of schooling, whether or not they are college bound.[3]

To meet this challenge, Dr. Adler recommends a variety of teaching techniques, which include the following:

- For the acquisition of knowledge there would be didactic instruction, lecturing, and textbooks in language, literature, fine arts, mathematics, natural science, history, geography, and social studies.
- For the development of intellectual skills and skills of learning, teachers would use coaching and supervised practice for the understanding of ideas and values.
- The Socratic questioning technique and active participation would be utilized. There would be ongoing discussion of books (not textbooks) and other works of art, including music, drama, and the visual arts.[4]

The suggestions included in this very traditional approach to education would be consistent with the recommendations of the *A Nation at Risk* report. The need to provide a challenging education for all children along with an emphasis on reading, writing, math, and science is present in most of the influential publications of the 80s. The criticism of the increased use of electives in high school is also present in a number of reports.

The anti-elective sentiment was included in a book published in 1983 by Ernest Boyer. This widely read volume did not suggest that all the electives should be ended but it did call for an increase in the number of required classes. Boyer's list of "basics" was longer than many other critics, but he agreed that all students should be in a single track and that we should end the practice of offering general and vocational tracks.[5]

In 1983 alone, there were eight studies published calling for a reform in our public schools. One of these was prepared by the Business–Higher Education Forum. Entitled *The American Competitive Challenge: The Need for Response*, it concluded emphatically that "a major reason for U.S. economic problems and falling productivity is the inadequate education of the nation's workers, who need more schooling in mathematics, science, critical-thinking skills and verbal expression." This document, like the *A Nation at Risk* report, was heavily affected by the worries of the business community.[6] With globalization and the increase in economic competition, the number of unskilled jobs in the

United States was declining rapidly as this work was being done in other countries. As assembly-line manufacturing jobs disappeared, employers demanded better-educated workers with competent basic skills and some technological sophistication. Many business leaders were complaining about the amount of training they were required to offer new employees, especially in the areas of communication skills and mathematics. Representatives for the business community suggested that the high school diploma signified very little.[7] Other reports echoed the need for schools to be improved if the United States was to remain competitive in the world. The National Task Force for Economic Growth report included these words:

> We have expected too little of our schools over the past two decades and we have gotten too little. The result is that our schools are not doing an adequate job of educating for today's requirements in the workplace, much less tomorrow's.[8]

A similar sentiment is expressed in the report of the Task Force on Elementary and Secondary Educational Policy, which states that "we think that they [the public schools] should ensure the availability of large numbers of skilled and capable individuals without whom we cannot sustain a complex and competitive economy."[9]

Also published in 1983 was a call to action by a task force of forty-one governors, legislators, labor leaders, business leaders, and school board members. The *Action For Excellence: A Comprehensive Plan to Improve Our Nation's Schools* report is consistent in many of its recommendations with the *A Nation at Risk* report. It called for better preparation and pay for teachers, stronger curriculum offerings (with standards), and greater school accountability.[10] Similar suggestions were included in still another report written in 1983 and prepared by a group of College Board members along with high school and college teachers. The recommendation of this committee called for a more rigorous preparation for college students through a more demanding curriculum beginning in the elementary school and continuing through high school. The *Academic Preparation for College: What Students Need to Know and Be Able to Do* report also calls for higher expectations for all students with appropriate remedial help for those children who are unable to keep up with their classmates. Here again the study calls for preparing better-trained teachers.[11]

Another idea that was included in the *A Nation at Risk* report is found in a document called *Educating America For the Twenty-First Century: A Report to the American People and the National Science Board*. This study, which was prepared by the National Science Board's Commission on Pre-College Education in Mathematics, Science, and Technology, not only emphasizes the need to improve instruction in science and math, but also suggests alternative teacher-training programs to encourage those already well prepared in these academic areas to enter the teaching profession.[12]

The calls for educational reform continued throughout the 1980s. In 1984, a study entitled *The Shopping Mall High School* underscored the need for involved parents, higher expectations for students, and preparing more effective teachers. The development of the teaching profession was also the focus in 1986 of the Task Force on Teaching as a Profession. This panel of educators, policymakers, and politicians called for the establishment of a National Board of Professional Teaching Standards to test and certify all teachers.[13] Although this initiative has yet to create a mandated national certification requirement for all teachers, it did lead to the formation in 1986 of the National Board for Professional Teaching Standards. This agency is now offering a national certification option to experienced teachers. "Board Certification" can be achieved by a teacher who has three years of teaching experience. Already more than sixteen thousand teachers nationwide have met the requirements for national certification.

Also in 1986, a group of deans of education departments and one college president released the so-called *Holmes Report*. This document also sought to improve the preparation of teachers by recommending that all candidates for certification first receive a bachelor's degree in an academic field and then earn a master's degree in education.[14] In another report issued by the National Governor's Association entitled *Time for Results*, there was a strong case for improving the teaching profession by instituting the idea of career ladders. The chairperson of the group, Lamar Alexander, who was at the time governor of Tennessee, was able to introduce such a plan in his home state and use it as a way to raise teacher salaries.[15] Perhaps of more historical significance was the report's support of the concept of school choice. Although this idea was not mentioned in *A Nation at Risk*, it would become one of the most important reform initiatives of the past two decades.

During the same year, Secretary of Education William Bennett issued a study called *First Lessons*, which added to the chorus calling for more emphasis on reading and other basic skills at the elementary school level. This was followed by a U.S. Department of Education publication called *James Madison High*, in which Secretary Bennett recommended "a traditional high school curriculum with few electives; four years of literature; a senior research paper; three years of math, science, and social studies with a United States and Western focus; and an emphasis on foreign language."[16]

A year later in 1987, E. D. Hirsh, a professor of English at the University of Virginia, published a best-selling book entitled *Cultural Literacy*. Reacting against the flexible curriculum that had evolved in many schools and also the growing emphasis on multicultural education, Hirsh recommends an "explicit" curriculum for all students. He goes so far as to create a "list of important names, dates, ideas, and allusions that all students should learn." This list would define "the basic vocabulary of our culture." After the success of the book, Hirsh and his colleagues have gone on to establish about one thousand schools which teach this so-called "core knowledge."[17] Although the idea of "core knowledge" was not discussed in the *A Nation at Risk* report, it is not inconsistent with the "back to basics" focus of most of the reform documents published during the 1980s.

The capstone reform effort of this period came with the issuance of *America 2000: An Educational Strategy*. Known as *Goals 2000*, this initiative was begun by President George H. W. Bush and was modified by President Clinton. As a result of an educational summit, including the nation's governors in 1989, six goals were established to be accomplished by the year 2000. These long-term objectives were as follows:

1. All children will start school ready to learn.
2. The high school graduation rate will increase to 90 percent.
3. All students in grades 4, 8, and 12 will demonstrate competency in English, math, science, civics and foreign language, economics, arts, history, and geography.
4. U.S. students will be first in math and science achievement.
5. Every adult will be literate.
6. Every school in the U.S. will be free of drugs and violence, and the unauthorized presence of firearms and alcohol.

In 1994, Congress added additional goals to improve the quality of teacher education and increase parental involvement in schools.[18]

Almost all of these goals were consistent with the aspirations outlined in *A Nation at Risk*. Thus, as the nation entered the 1990s, it would seem that a consensus on the agenda for reform had been established. Although it might have appeared that there was universal acceptance of the steps necessary to improve our schools, there were a number of critics who felt that the direction of the reform movement was inappropriate.

There were those who did not accept the premise that our schools were failing. These critics would debate the data used in the various reports as well as the recommendations that were put forth. Others said that the primary problem was the lack of equal opportunity in the current system. These individuals believed that the first priority should be to provide adequate funding for our urban and rural schools. For them, the problem was primarily rooted in the way we finance public education. A third group felt that the focus on traditional teaching and "back to basics" is not what is needed for the twenty-first century. These individuals would emphasize the importance of developing students who were critical thinkers rather than young people who could merely restate information on a standardized test. In order to understand what has happened in our schools during the past twenty years, it is necessary to consider all of the major participants in our national debate on schools. At this point it would seem helpful to turn to those who were outside of the consensus.

NOTES

1. Beatrice Gross and Ronald Gross, eds., *The School Debate* (New York: Simon & Schuster, 1985), 186.

2. Kevin Ryan and James Cooper, *Those Who Can, Teach* (Boston: Houghton Mifflin, 1988), 78, 180.

3. Kevin Ryan and James Cooper, *Kaleidoscope: Readings in Education* (Boston: Houghton Mifflin, 2004), 66.

4. Ryan and Cooper, *Kaleidoscope*, 167.

5. Myra Pollack Sadker and David Miller Sadker, *Teachers, Schools, and Society* (McGraw-Hill, 2003), 233.

6. Sadker and Sadker, *Teachers, Schools, and Society*, app. A, pp. 8–9.

7. Diane Ravitch, *Left Back: A Century of Battles Over School Reform* (New York: Touchstone, 2000), 429–30.

8. Gross and Gross, *The School Debate*, 364.

9. Gross and Gross, *The School Debate*, 364.

10. Congressional Research Service, *Should More Rigorous Academic Standards Be Established For All Public Elementary and/or Secondary Schools in the United States?* (Library of Congress, 1985), 58–60.

11. Sadker and Sadker, *Teachers, Schools, and Society*, app. A, pp. 8–9.

12. Sadker and Sadker, *Teachers, Schools, and Society*, app. A, pp. 8–9.

13. Sadker and Sadker, *Teachers, Schools, and Society*, app. A, pp. 10–11.

14. James Wm. Noll, *Taking Sides: Clashing Views on Controversial Educational Issues* (Guilford: McGraw-Hill, 2004), 378–79.

15. Gross, *The School Debate*, 481–82.

16. Sadker and Sadker, *Teachers, Schools, and Society*, app. A, p. 11.

17. Ravitch, *Left Back*, 419–20.

18. Jack L. Nelson, Stuart B. Palonsky, and Mary Rose McCarthy, *Critical Issues in Education: Dialogues and Dialectics* (Boston: McGraw-Hill, 2004), 153.

CHAPTER 5

The Critics

Although the initial reaction of the media to the *A Nation at Risk* report was for the most part enthusiastic, the document did have its critics. During the first month after its release, it was the subject of twenty-eight stories in the *Washington Post*. Even in this influential paper, columnist Joseph Kraft excoriates "conservatives for using the report to beat up on liberals without offering anything constructive."[1] Conservative guru William Buckley suggested that the recommendations were so unimaginative that they could have originated from a phone conversation between any two intelligent people. He went on to label the report as being "banal" because it called for nothing new. Also in the *New York Times*, Peter Applebome called the report "brilliant propaganda." Russell Baker, the *Times* humor columnist, "contended that a sentence containing a phrase like 'a rising tide of mediocrity' wouldn't be worth more than a C in tenth-grade English." About the authors' writing overall, Baker said, "I'm giving them an A+ in mediocrity."[2]

In responding to the premise of the *A Nation at Risk* report that schools were responsible for our nation's lackluster economic performance, respected historian Lawrence Cremin wrote the following:

> American economic competitiveness with Japan and other nations is to a considerable degree a function of monetary, trade, and industrial policy, and of decisions made by the President and Congress, the Federal Reserve Board, and the Federal Departments of the Treasury, Commerce, and Labor. Therefore, to conclude that problems of international competitiveness can be solved by educational reform, especially educational reform defined solely as school reform, is not merely utopian and mil-

lenialist, it is at best a foolish and at worst a crass effort to direct attention away from those truly responsible for doing something about com-
petitiveness and to lay the burden instead upon schools. It is a device that
has been used repeatedly in the history of American education.[3]

A significant number of educators also attacked the statistics used by
the Commission to reach their conclusions. One of the primary critics
of the report was Gerald Bracey, who has written that the report "is a
golden treasury of selective and spun statistics." In an article entitled,
"The Propaganda of 'A Nation at Risk,'" he includes rebuttals to the
"indicators" contained in the report. One problem cited was the decline
in science achievement test scores of seventeen-year-old students in the
United States. Bracey suggests that this decline made it into the report
because it was the only one of nine trend lines that showed a dramatic
decrease. He points out that the science scores of nine- and thirteen-
year-olds were, "if anything . . . inching up." In addition he questions
the assertion in the report stating that "international comparisons of student achievement completed a decade ago, reveal that on 19 academic
tests, American students were never first or second and, in comparison
with other industrialized nations, were last 7 times." Bracey claims that
these studies all had "fundamental methodological flaws" and that the
Commission could have chosen other questionable studies to prove that
"American kids are above average in science, average in math, and second in the world in reading."[4]

A number of critics believed that the use of lower scores on the
Scholastic Assessment Test as an indicator of decline was also unfair.
Even though it is obvious that the scores were declining before the year
1983, critics pointed out that many more students were taking these exams. Two decades earlier, when only a minority of students went on to
college, only the top academic students took these tests. With the number of those seeking admission to college in the 80s growing rapidly,
the average scores were affected by the fact that many less able high
school seniors were taking the exam. On the positive side, the trend for
poor and minority students was moving upward.[5]

It is also true that the Scholastic Assessment Test does not purport to
test our knowledge in fields such as history and science. The purpose is
rather to measure a student's aptitude to succeed in college. As a result,

it has been pointed out that it does not measure how well schools have prepared students academically.

Another major concern of a number of professional educators was that the report created an unfair "sense of doom" about our schools, rather than a "balanced assessment." These critics would point to the fact that even at the time of the study leading up to the *A Nation at Risk* report, as a society, we lacked the necessary research sources and did not have sufficient data to either critically judge our schools or develop the appropriate solutions to educational problems. One of the by-products of the various reports has been a serious effort, especially by the Federal Department of Education, to carry out major studies on the academic progress of students at all levels. Still, criticism continues on the way the government has handled educational data during the past two decades. Critics of public education blamed schools for the recession in the early 80s, but no government study gave schools any credit for the economic boom of the 90s. Soon after the *New York Times* declared that our economy was again number one in the world, Lou Gerstner, the chairman of the board at IBM, wrote in the same paper an article entitled *Our Schools are Failing*. Some critics have gone so far as to charge the federal government with hiding indicators of good news about our schools. One such critic is Gerald W. Bracey, who wrote in the *Phi Delta Kappan* about one such situation:

> The most egregious example of suppression—that we know about—was the suspension of the Sandia report. Assembled in 1990 by engineers at Sandia National laboratories in Albuquerque, the report presented seventeen pages of graphs and tables and seventy-eight pages of text to explain them. It concluded that, while there were many problems in public education, there was no systemwide crisis. Secretary of Energy James Watkins, who was asked for the report, called it "dead wrong" in the *Albuquerque Journal*. Briefed by the Sandia engineers who compiled it, Deputy Secretary of Education and former Xerox CEO David Kearns told them, "you bury this or I'll bury you." The engineers were forbidden to leave New Mexico to discuss the report. Officially, according to Diane Ravitch, then assistant secretary of education, the report was undergoing "peer review" by other agencies (an unprecedented occurrence) and was not ready for publication.
>
> Lee Bray, the Vice President of Sandia, supervised the engineers who produced the report. I asked Bray, now retired, about the fate of the report. He affirmed that it was definitely and deliberately suppressed.[6]

It is only a conjecture, but it is possible that some officials in the education department did not want to slow the momentum for change by announcing any good news.

Others who criticized the *A Nation at Risk* report charged that it was using "dated information" and "comparing comprehensive American schools with limited-population elite schools in Germany and Japan."[7] Still another of the indictors included in the report was that "23 million American adults are functionally illiterate by the simplistic test of everyday reading." Lawrence C. Stedman and Marshall S. Smith point out in an article entitled "Weak Arguments, Poor Data, Simplistic Recommendations" that

> apart from the problem of defining "literacy" at any given moment in history, and that the definition has changed over time to become more rigorous as society has changed its demands, it is clear from almost every recent report that the problem of illiteracy for young adults is very heavily concentrated in the poor and minority (particularly male) population, a fact that goes unmentioned in the report.[8]

In summarizing the comments concerning the data used by the Commission on Excellence, these authors believe that the case for a serious "decline" in our educational programs "though rhetorically compelling" was based on

> weak arguments and poor data to make their case. Neither the decline in test scores, the international comparisons, nor the growth of high-tech employment provided a clear rationale for reform. By ignoring their background reports and carelessly handling data, their reports further lost credibility. In particular the commissions made simplistic recommendations and failed to consider their ramifications.[9]

While some critics challenged the data, others suggested that most of the reform reports were focusing on the wrong problems. In his bestselling book *Savage Inequalities*, Jonathan Kozol graphically highlights the lack of equal educational opportunity in the United States. In the book he argues that "under-financed public schools in poor areas make a mockery of democratic ideals."[10] Kozol credits the *A Nation at Risk* report for its recognition of some of the problems facing public education but believes that "its single-minded emphasis on military needs and on commercial competition was myopic."[11] For this critic at least, the primary answers to the issues raised in the report will not come from Washington. They will be provided in our communities and neighborhoods. The "enemy remains our own shortsighted sense of class advantage at the cost of national well-being and of universal humane competence in service of survival."[12] He would point to the truly unequal way we finance education in the United States. This case would be bolstered by some statistics distributed in New York State that show the amount of money being spent on students in four different school districts. Based on spending in the year 2000–2001 the Port Jefferson District on Long Island was spending $16,668 for the education of each student while a student in Nyack, a blue-collar suburb of New York City would be given an education costing $9,851. The Niagara Falls District (a small city in upstate New York) was spending $7,291 during the same year that the Sherburne–Earlville School District in central New York was spending $4,973 per pupil.[13] For Kozol, it is inequalities such as these that should be the first priority for educational reform. As a spokesman for the teaching profession, he and other critics have also expressed serious doubts about the reforms called for by the *A Nation at Risk* report. John Goodlad writes about the reactions of the public to the solutions highlighted in the report:

> Over the past year, I have been asking members of groups to which I speak to select from four items the one they believe to have the most promise for improving our schools. . . .
>
> - Standards and tests mandated by all states;
> - A qualified, competent teacher in every classroom;
> - Non-promotion and grade retention for all students who fail to reach grade level standards on the tests;
> - Schools of choice for all parents.
>
> From an audience of about one thousand people at the 2001 National School Boards Association Conference, one person chose the first. All the rest chose the second, which usually is the unanimous choice, whatever the group.[14]

Curriculum standards were undoubtedly one of the by-products of the reform movements of the 80s. For some, these standards were the result of a "manufactured crisis." These critics believed that the bad news featured in these documents presented the opportunity for those on the right in religion and politics to take control of schools. One liberal writer has observed that

> only with national and statewide curricula could ultraconservatives be assured that disquieting local voices—advocates of gay rights, abortion rights, and birth control, for example—could be kept out of schools. Other more centrist conservatives wanted schools to return to the "good old days," before they had been captured by "social experimentalists," advocates of whole language, new math, and sex education in schools. . . . The publication of *A Nation at Risk* not only fueled the myth of failing schools, it paved the way for a conservative reform agenda and business solutions to educational problems.[15]

With the imposition of what some critics saw as narrow and confining curriculum standards, it seemed inevitable that "high-stakes" tests would be encouraged to ensure that these standards were actually being taught. The new tests would then be used to enforce a new accountability for our schools. Kozol and Goodlad, along with many others, have forcefully argued that "high-stakes" testing will not solve our educational problems, especially among our most disadvantaged children. Merely raising the bar does not help children to jump higher. More than one educator has observed that schools should use alternative means of assessment. They should consider "a rich portfolio of papers, essays, videos, poems, photographs, drawings, and tape-recorded answers, not a series of test scores."[16]

Others who criticized the report said that it was almost totally focused on high schools. A task force established by the Carnegie Foundation emphasized the need to improve our junior high schools or middle schools. This report talked about the students in these schools experiencing periods of "significant physical, social, and psychological change." It goes on to recommend that young adolescents be in smaller learning communities, have a core curriculum, eliminate academic grouping, develop programs to improve students' self-esteem, and improve school–community–parent relationships.[17]

As a result of this report and other studies, the 1980s became a time when many school districts reorganized their programs by replacing junior high schools (buildings housing grades 7, 8, and 9) with middle schools (housing grades 6, 7, and 8). For these districts, junior high schools had become like a "mini high school." Students jumped immediately from a self-contained sixth-grade classroom where they were exposed to primarily one teacher to a junior high, where they moved to a new teacher's classroom every forty-five minutes. Especially in large buildings, students could find it difficult to form meaningful relationships with adults.

Middle schools were developed to provide a more comfortable transition from elementary school to high school. Teaching styles were to be more "student centered" rather than the "teacher-centered" classes in most high schools. Student activity evenings featuring games replaced dances in darkened gymnasiums. Serious efforts were made to allow middle school students to bond with their teachers. In some ways, the goals of the middle school movement differed from the objectives of the reforms that emerged from the *A Nation at Risk* and other reports. By the turn of the century, conservative critics were criticizing middle schools for a lack of academic rigor. Although this movement in the 80s and 90s even caused some states to develop a special certification category for middle school teachers, the momentum for new middle schools may well be slowed by the worries over test scores.

The century-long debate between those who support the traditional academic curriculum and teaching methods and those who call for innovations featuring student-centered learning did not cease during the 80s and 90s. In the tradition of John Dewey and other progressives, John Holt was a spokesman for the critics of traditional teacher-centered learning when he wrote

> Most children in school fail. . . . They fail because they are afraid, bored, and confused . . . bored because the things they are given and told to do in school are so trivial, so dull, and make such limited and narrow demands on the wide spectrum of their intelligence, capabilities, and talents. . . . Schools should be a place where children learn what they want to know, instead of what we think they ought to know.[18]

Several other individuals whose ideas were contrary to the consensus during the last third of the twentieth century were Paulo Freire and Ivan Illich. Freire maintained that "students should not be manipulated or controlled but should be involved in their own learning." This could be done by "exchanging and examining their experience with peers and mentors." For Illich, the answer to our educational problems could not be solved by schools as we now know them. In his book *Deschooling Society*, he calls for a total political and educational revolution.[19]

For the most part, the voices of the critics were not heard by the general public. During the past twenty years, most Americans accepted the notion that our schools needed to be improved and that the remedy of standards, high-stakes testing, and accountability offered an appropriate solution. As we now begin to look back on these two decades, one can hope that we are on the right path to bring about improvement in our schools. It is also hoped that a review of the trends that had dominated public education will help us to answer the question, are we still a nation at risk after two decades? We begin this examination by looking at one of the key elements in our reform movement, the establishment of curriculum standards.

NOTES

1. Gerald W. Bracey, "April Foolishness: The 20th Anniversary of a Nation at Risk," *Phi Delta Kappan*, April 2003, www.pdkintl.org/kappan/k0304bra .htm (accessed 7 October 2003).

2. Bracey, "April Foolishness."

3. Lawrence J. Cremin, *Popular Education and Its Discontents* (New York: Harper & Row, 1989), 102–103.

4. Gerald Bracey, "The Propaganda of 'A Nation at Risk,'" *Education Disinformation Detection and Reporting Agency*, 15 September 1999, www.america-tomorrow.com/bracey/EDDRA/EDDRA8.htm (accessed 29 August 2003).

5. Ray Marshall and Marc Tucker, *Thinking for a Living: Education and the Wealth of Nations* (New York: Basic Books, 1992), 77.

6. Bracey, "April Foolishness." (The report finally appeared in full in 1993 in the May/June issue of the *Journal of Educational Research* under the title "Perspectives on Education in America.")

7. John D. Pulliam and James Van Patten, *History of Education in America* (Englewood Cliffs: Prentice Hall, 1991), 198.

8. Beatrice Gross and Ronald Gross, eds., *The Great School Debate* (New York: Simon & Schuster, 1985), 85.

9. Gross and Gross, *The Great School Debate*, 102.

10. Jack L. Nelson, Stuart B. Palonsky, and Mary Rose McCarthy, *Critical Issues in Education: Dialogues and Dialectics* (Boston: McGraw-Hill, 2004), 203.

11. Jonathan Kozol, *Illiterate America* (New York: Anchor Press/Doubleday, 1985), 74.

12. Jonathan Kozol, *Illiterate America*, 79.

13. Midstate School Finance Consortium, "Unfortunately, Some Kids Don't Get It" (poster published by the Midstate School Finance Consortium, data supplied by the New York State Department of Education, 2000–2001).

14. Nelson, Palonsky, and McCarthy, *Critical Issues in Education*, 159.

15. Nelson, Palonsky, and McCarthy, *Critical Issues in Education*, 160.

16. Nelson, Palonsky, and McCarthy, *Critical Issues in Education*, 362.

17. Myra Pollack Sadker and David Miller Sadker, *Teachers, Schools, and Society* (McGraw-Hill, 2003), app. A, p. 11.

18. J. Holt, *How Children Fail* (New York: Pitman, 1964), xiii, xiv, 174.

19. L. Dean Webb, Arlene Metha, and K. Forbis Jordan, *Foundations of American Education* (Upper Saddle River: Prentice-Hall, 2000), 121.

CHAPTER 6

The Standards

"We recommend that schools, colleges, and universities adopt more rigorous and measurable standards, and higher expectations, for academic performance."[1] During the 1980s these words in the *A Nation at Risk* report, along with similar recommendations from other commissions, politicians, and most especially business leaders, helped to foster what has become known as the standards movement. Actually, the word *standards* has two separate meanings in public discussions concerning schools. One connotation is that we need to raise our academic expectations for students. In other words, we must ask more of them. The other meaning attached to the standards movement deals with developing specific curriculum objectives in every subject area. It is this aspect of the standards movement that we consider in this chapter. Simply put, these curriculum standards are an attempt to articulate what students should know and be able to do as a result of their education in a specific curriculum area. As important as the establishment of these more demanding educational objectives is the companion assumption that *all* children could and should seek to master these higher standards.

It is important to note that the standards include not only what are called "content standards" (what students should know) but also "performance standards" which "describe what level of performance is good enough for students to be described as advanced, proficient, below basic, or some other performance level."[2]

The current campaign to write demanding curriculum standards did not occur directly after the published reports in the early 80s. For many states, the initial reforms were centered on increasing the number of academic core classes required for high school graduation. In many states, the number of science and math classes mandated for all students was increased along with new foreign language requirements. Historian Diane Ravitch gives credit to the president of the American Federation of Teachers, Albert Shanker, for his crucial influence in the discussions on how to improve the quality of our schools. Throughout the 1990s until his death in 1997, he argued in speeches and in his regular column in the *New York Times* that standards were too low. He said that "schools needed high standards as well as rigorous tests that had real consequences or 'stakes' for students, such as getting into college or a good job training program."[3] Speaking to the Governor's Conference in 1989, Shanker called for establishing a national system of standards and assessment.

At this same conference, the state leaders agreed to six national goals for the year 2000. Bill Clinton, who chaired the meeting, followed through with this project after he became president, when he instructed his Department of Education to establish a commission to develop voluntary standards in seven curriculum areas. In 1994, legislation was introduced that also provided funds to state governments for developing curriculum standards and assessments. There was a serious political difference in Washington and in the country at large as to whether these standards should be uniform throughout the nation or if each state should devise its own. After the Republicans gained control of both houses of Congress in 1994, a federal board established earlier to evaluate standards developed at both the national and state levels was abolished by Congress. With standards being written at both levels, the debate became intense. The national history standards drawn up by the National Center for History in the Schools raised a chorus of objections from prominent critics. Lynne Cheney, the wife of Vice President Richard Cheney, who herself had held the important position as chairperson of the National Endowment for the Humanities, criticized the history standards for being much too negative in their choice of topics. She noted that Senator Joseph McCarthy was mentioned nineteen times and the Ku Klux Klan seventeen times. Harriet Tubman's name was included six times, while there was no mention of Paul Revere, Robert E. Lee, Thomas Alva Edison, Alexander Graham Bell, or the Wright brothers. Her comments set off a spirited debate among educators and historians, as well as in the media.[4]

Although the authors of the report fought back, the proposed national standards for history demonstrated the difficulty of reaching an agreement on a specific list of national curriculum objectives. This problem, along with the consistent preference of most Republicans that education remain a function of state and local government, resulted in fifty separate sets of state standards. Another reason for the failure of the effort to establish one set of curriculum standards for the entire nation is that such an approach "contradicted the rationale for school choice," a concept that was becoming increasingly popular during the 90s. For those who wished schools "to operate in a free market atmosphere," national curriculum standards and testing would be too restrictive. Although a report of the U.S. Department of Education entitled *America 2000* did call for both the option of school choice and national curriculum standards, the sentiment for state and local control has, at least for the present, carried the day.[5]

The standards movement began in earnest with the National Education Summit in 1996. Organized by Louis Gerstner, this session included most of the state governors, prominent business leaders, as well as President Clinton.[6] With the strong support of business leaders and state-level politicians, by the end of the 1990s, forty-nine states and the District of Columbia had developed a list of standards for all major curriculum areas. Even though they are now the centerpieces of education in the United States, the debate on the merits of the standards movement continues. Those who are convinced of the absolute need for clear curriculum standards were undoubtedly affected by the *A Nation at Risk* report. It has become widely accepted that other societies that do have clearly articulated educational objectives have surpassed U.S. students in numerous comparative studies. As we began the decade of the 1980s, many educators also believed that our schools did not have high academic expectations for all students. In every state, significant numbers of students were following programs designed for those who did not plan to go to college. The requirements, especially in math and science, were limited.

Supporters of the standards movement pointed to the fact that our system of local control allowed individual administrators and school boards to provide programs that did not challenge students academically. For those who believed that this was the case, the standards movement could "end local parochialism and broaden students' horizons." For others, "a common set of standards promotes cooperation. Teachers and principals will work together to identify problems, develop instructional solutions,

and collaborate as a professional team working to ensure that all standards are met."[7]

For business leaders, the primary benefit of standards would be that
they provided "measurable goals." Many from the business community
voiced the opinion that public schools lacked a vision for what needed
to be accomplished. They also believed that without standards, no one
could be held accountable for failure or success. These critics argued
that for far too long individual schools had been allowed to "do their
own thing." For those supporting curriculum standards, this laissez-
faire approach to education had to change so that schools could at least
have a basis to measure what they were doing. For the business professionals who supported standards, such reform was absolutely necessary if we were to have technically competent workers who could help
our industries compete in world markets. Those with this point of view
believed that failure to do so would have an extremely negative effect
on the standard of living in this country.[8]

In addition, a number of educators suggested that standards would
aid teachers by providing clear-cut guidelines as to what should be
taught. Too often, local curriculums were centered around a textbook or
workbook. As a result, it was the publisher of these books who actually
was determining the curriculum. The best standards would not be totally inflexible but would at least identify the desired educational outcomes. Individual schools, academic departments, and instructors
would still have the latitude to determine the exact content and also the
teaching methods to be utilized. Many teachers welcomed the guidelines established by the state standards. Some instructors were even
grateful for the additional challenge created by the high stake tests,
which were developed to measure students' success in meeting the
standards.

Those who championed academic curriculum standards point out
that the process used to develop these goals was more thorough and effective than would have ever been possible at the local level. Educators, parents, sometimes business leaders, and even students were involved in the exhaustive process of creating state standards. Because
state governments were able to expend the necessary funds, experts in
each academic area were used as consultants and commission members
in creating the standards. Once drafts of the new standards had been
completed, discussions occurred in many states involving teachers and

community members. When this process was followed, these public hearings often led to revisions in the original proposal. The tests that resulted from the standards movement also, in many states, were carefully devised. Experts in testing were used along with teachers and college professors in an attempt to ensure that the test really did evaluate how effectively the standards were being met.[9]

Initially it was very difficult for educators to quarrel with the idea of standards or the new tests. To do so could give the impression that schools were afraid of becoming accountable. Journalist John Merrow suggested that criticizing standards is like "booing Mom or the American flag." Although he has reservations about much of what is happening in the name of educational reform, he agrees that standards "make sense," especially when 20 percent of American families move every year. At least those who move within a state have a better chance of making a transition from school to school if there are state standards.[10]

The most important result of the standards movement for many is the fact that it attempts to provide equal opportunity for all students. In doing so it helps to ensure a school experience that is "decidedly coherent, if not predictable."[11] The popularity of the movement is illustrated by the fact that it has remained a primary cornerstone of educational reform in the United States for at least a dozen years. It would appear that public support has been quite consistent during this time period.

> According to a public opinion poll by the Business Round Table, a Washington, D.C.-based coalition of corporate CEO's, a majority of the American public believes that the effort to adopt standards is "very much" a move in the right direction. According to an *Education Week* survey in 2000, 39 percent of teachers say that raising standards for what students should learn each year is "very much" a move in the right direction; 48 percent say it is a move that is "somewhat" in the right direction.[12]

Even with this support, there have been numerous cautions raised by those who fear the current direction of the standards movement.

Critics who have studied the standards developed by individual states have commented that some are so vague that practically any standardized test could measure the results. In these states, some teachers complain that the standards are not particularly helpful in determining what should be taught as students are prepared for the high stake test in their state. Other states have written standards that are very specific as to exactly what should be taught at each grade level.[13] In states such as Virginia, teachers are told exactly which historical figures must be considered in social studies classes at every grade level. Attempts have been made to describe an effective learning standard. Such an effort was published in 1998 in a study by Finn, Petrilli, and Vanourek. Below are two examples of what these researchers consider as outstanding learning standards:

Example of a Skills-Based Standard

The student should 1) Locate main ideas in multiple types of sources (e.g., nonprint, specialized references, periodicals, newspapers, atlases, yearbooks, government publications, etc.); 2) Take notes and develop outlines through reading, listening, or viewing; 3) Use features of books for information: table of contents, glossary, index, appendix, bibliography; 4) Distinguish between fact and opinion relating to regions/cultures. (Georgia standards, grade 7, social studies skills)[14]

Example of a Knowledge-Based Standard

The student will identify the sources and describe the development of democratic principles in Western Europe and the United States. . . . After examining major documents (such as the Declaration of Independence, the Constitution of the United States, the English Bill of Rights, the Declaration of the Rights of Man, or the Universal Declaration of Human Rights) for specific democratic principles they contain, the student makes a comparison chart showing how certain principles appear in these documents. (California standards, standard 3, Grade 10)[15]

In the same survey, the authors ranked the standards of those states that had adopted their own curriculum standards by 1998. Their findings listed the standards of the state of Arizona as the best in the nation. This was followed by California and Texas. Nine states were given an F for their standards.[16] An example of failing standards in the study would be those of New York for the areas of history and geography.

Standard 1: History of the United States and New York
    Students will use a variety of intellectual skills to demonstrate their understanding of major ideas, eras, themes, developments, and turning points in the history of the United States and New York.

Standard 3: Geography
  Students will use a variety of intellectual skills to demonstrate their understanding of the geography of the interdependent world in which we live—local, national, and global—including the distribution of people, places, and environments over the Earth's surface.[17]

Although these two single sentences used in New York do appear to be so general in nature that they would offer little help to teachers, it is also true that the New York State Education Department has provided additional documents and an Internet site to help teachers meet the standards in their classroom. Even with these additional sources, the information is not specific enough for many teachers. The fact is that the American Federation of Teachers in their annual report *Making Standards Matter*, "found that only five states have standards that are clear and specific for all four major subject areas at the elementary, middle, and high school levels."[18] There has also been considerable discussion over the level of difficulty of the standards that have been adopted in various states. While three-quarters of the teachers quizzed in one survey believe that the expectations were "about right," only 42 percent of the parents agreed. A slight majority of these parents apparently thought that the standards were not demanding enough.[19]

  The way that decisions have been made regarding state standards has also bothered some critics. In most states, committees or commissions have been formed with representatives from colleges and universities, classroom teachers, and sometimes parents and others outside of the education field. These groups are selected and guided by representatives of the state education departments. Separate task forces are usually set up for each subject area. Arriving at a proper mix of individuals is always a challenge. Teacher groups expect to be in the majority, although this does not always happen. In a field such as social studies, there is serious interest within the academic disciplines of history, political science, sociology, economics, geography, and possibly psychology and anthropology. Academics representing each of these fields are anxious to have input into what is taught in social studies classes. For standards developed for business and vocational education, representatives of the business community should be involved. Health and physical education standards also draw a number of interested groups. There are religious organizations that are concerned about the curriculum content involving birth control and abortion. Also there are antidrug and alcohol organizations that wish to use the school curriculum to forward their group objectives.

Especially for teachers and professors, the process of establishing curriculum standards is a serious business. These groups need to be given sufficient time and resources to support their work. Even with excellent staffing and research capabilities, the committees can become divided and experience great difficulty in reaching a consensus. When they finally do publish their recommendations, the authors should be ready for an onslaught of criticism. Even after the formal adoption, state governments need to be prepared for periodic reevaluation and amendment of their standards.

For some, the standards and the companion movements for high-stakes testing and school accountability are a source of concern and even anger. Such a reaction is contained in a book entitled *The Manufactured Crisis*, written by David Berliner and Bruce Biddle. These authors suggested what some might call a conspiracy theory by politicians and business leaders to "scapegoat educators." Berliner and Biddle believe that

> some of those who have accepted hostile myths about education have been genuinely worried about our schools, some have misunderstood evidence, some have been duped, and some have had understandable reasons for their actions. But many of the myths seem to have been told by powerful people who—despite their protestations—were pursuing a political agenda designed to weaken the nation's public schools, redistribute support for those schools so that privileged students are favored over needy students, or even abolish those schools altogether. To this end they have been prepared to tell lies, suppress evidence, scapegoat educators, and sow endless confusion. We consider this conduct particularly despicable.[20]

For these outraged educators, the standards movement and what has followed has merely masked the true problems facing education. For them, the real issues include the failure of our system to provide equal educational opportunity; the growing income inequities in our society that maintain a large class of poor people, even among those who hold jobs; and the lack of effective parenting in the lives of many children. A standardized state curriculum does not solve these problems that represent the true underlying difficulties faced in many of our schools. Pressuring teachers who are already overwhelmed to meet more difficult curriculum standards will not in itself improve education in America.

Many of these same critics charged that the standards are reducing teaching and learning to merely a list of "measurable skills." In Tennessee for instance, the Education Department has written that they have broken learning into "manageable, measurable bits." Some standards have been written in a way that can be "readily measured by multiple choice tests." When this type of approach is adopted to produce standards, textbook publishers must take notice, and as a result, as researcher Harriet Tyson-Bernstein has written in a book entitled *A Conspiracy of Good Intentions: America's Textbook Fiasco*, textbooks are increasingly a "mélange of test-oriented trivia."[21]

Supporters of the current reform movement counter that critics are merely looking for excuses to oppose needed change. In a book written by Abigail and Stephan Therenstrom entitled *No Excuses*, the authors point to what they see as "roadblocks to change." These include teachers' unions, school administrators who "lack energy and ambition" to bring about reform, and teachers the authors label as either "saints, masochists, or low-aspiring civil servants."[22]

Perhaps the most often-heard criticism of the standards movement is that it alone cannot increase academic growth among students. Even with the added motivation of high-stakes testing and school accountability, the key factor is what is happening in individual classrooms. The fact that all schools have similar curriculum goals and higher expectations will not matter unless teachers are able to do things differently with their students. In the words of one authority who doubts the current direction of school reform, "one would have to look far and wide to find evidence that standardization brings up bottom-scoring students."[23]

The debate over standards will continue. There is no question that the state standards that were agreed upon during the past decade will need to be revisited and hopefully improved. There are a number of conclusions that one might reach in attempting to evaluate the standards movement during the past decade. The vast majority of educators would concede that there was a need to improve our schools in 1983 when the *A Nation at Risk* report was published. Most would agree that at that time many students were not being adequately prepared to live their adult lives in the twenty-first century. As the percentage of students attending college increased, it became increasingly necessary to raise the academic requirements for those who were currently not enrolled in college entrance curriculums. Academic expectations were lower for those who were enrolled in the "general curriculum" or as business majors. Certainly those labeled as having learning disabilities or other handicapping conditions were not expected to succeed in an academic college entrance program. Thus, a strong argument could be made for the need to raise the academic expectation for a significant number of students.

It is because of this consensus that our nation has supported the development of curriculum standards. Despite the cautions expressed by a number of educators, some of whom have been very critical, states have standardized their curriculums in a short period of time. This process has in almost all cases been followed by a program of examinations designed to evaluate the success of schools in reaching the goals established by the standards. In 2002, with the passage of the *No Child Left Behind* legislation, such testing was made mandatory in grades 3–8. While the curriculum standards themselves have been accepted by most people, numerous critics have questioned the imposition of these new testing programs. It is this controversial issue, which also grew out of a recommendation of the *A Nation at Risk* report, that we will consider next.

NOTES

1. U.S. Department of Education, The National Commission on Excellence in Education, *A Nation at Risk: The Imperative for Educational Reform*, April 1983, Recommendations, 3.

2. Kathryn M. Doherty, "Standards," *Education Week*, 29 October 2003, www.edweek.org/context/topics/issuespage.cfm?id=55 (accessed 13 November 2003).

3. Diane Ravitch, *Left Back: A Century of Battles Over School Reform* (New York: Touchstone, 2000), 431.

4. Ravitch, *Left Back*, 434.

5. Peter S. Hlebowitsh, *Foundations of American Education* (Toronto: Wadsworth, 2001), 543–44.

6. John Merrow, *Choosing Excellence* (Lanham, MD: Scarecrow Press, 2001), 29.

7. Myra Pollack Sadker and David Miller Sadker, *Teachers, Schools, and Society* (McGraw-Hill, 2003), 272.

8. Sadker and Sadker, *Teachers, Schools, and Society*, 272.

9. Kevin Ryan and James Cooper, *Kaleidoscope: Readings in Education* (Boston: Houghton Mifflin, 2004), 161.

10. Merrow, *Choosing Excellence*, 28.

11. Hlebowitsh, *Foundations of American Education*, 546.

12. Doherty, "Standards."

13. David T. Gordon, ed., *A Nation Reformed?* (Cambridge, MA: Harvard Education Press, 2003), 146.

14. Hlebowitsh, *Foundations of American Education*, 550.

15. Hlebowitsh, *Foundations of American Education*, 550.

16. Hlebowitsh, *Foundations of American Education*, 546–47.

17. New York State Education Department, www.highered.nysed.gov/.

18. Doherty, "Standards."

19. Doherty, "Standards."

20. Davis C. Berliner and Bruce J. Biddle, *The Manufactured Crisis* (Reading, MA: Addison-Wesley Publishing, 1995), xii.

21. Harriet Tyson-Bernstein, *A Conspiracy of Good Intentions: America's Textbook Fiasco* (Washington D.C.: Council for Basic Education, May 1988).

22. Abigail Therenstrom and Stephan Therenstrom, *No Excuses* (New York: Simon & Schuster, 2003), 251–64.

23. Jack L. Nelson, Stuart B. Palonsky, and Mary Rose McCarthy, *Critical Issues in Education: Dialogues and Dialectics* (Boston: McGraw-Hill, 2004), 165.

CHAPTER 7

The Tests

For many reform leaders, especially those representing the business community, it was not enough to merely develop curriculum objectives or standards for the subjects taught in our schools. In order to ensure that students were actually mastering these standards, there had to be an efficient way to measure student learning. For those charged with the responsibility of providing an evaluation tool, the most obvious, simplest, and objective measurement method would be the traditional test. It was also important to make certain that students take these tests seriously, and therefore it was necessary to make the results of the tests meaningful to both students and school personnel. What students most care about are their grades, whether they will be promoted to the next level, receive a high school diploma, and be accepted at a college. What has become known as "high-stakes tests" have been introduced in every state to ensure that the curriculum standards are being efficiently and effectively taught.

There is a second major reason for the introduction of these tests. It was the consensus of opinion of those attempting to bring about educational reform during the 80s and the 90s that the results of these tests had to be important to school boards, administrators, and, most of all, teachers. This objective was premised on the idea that in order for the standards to be taken seriously, there had to be rewards and consequences for school districts and individual schools. Once again it was in part because of the urging of representatives of the business community that the concept of "accountability" for schools became an essential aspect of educational reform. Thus, in state after state, policies or laws were adopted which required that the results of the high-stakes test be disseminated to the public. Local newspapers along with radio and television stations were given detailed data comparing test results in districts across the state. Front-page stories highlighted the successes and failures of districts on the various tests. Often this information would include the pattern of the results for individual districts over a period of time. If a school failed to improve, it became obvious to the parents and citizens. In some states, schools are required to publish the comparative results in school newsletters. These publications are often more widely read than the local newspapers. In districts where the comparative scores remain near the bottom in their area, there is bound to be pressure on the board of education, the administrators, and the teachers to find a way to improve the test scores. There is general agreement that efforts to bring about increased accountability have indeed affected students, teachers, and other school officials. Prior to attempting to discern the impact of these trends, it perhaps would be helpful to consider the historic practice of giving tests to students.

Needless to say, teachers have given written tests to students since schools were formed. The possible reasons for testing are varied. One of the most positive reasons for giving examinations is to determine what students have learned as a result of instruction during a specific period of time. The test can be a "pop quiz" on a reading or homework assignment, a test on a unit of study, or a midterm examination. From the results, a teacher can determine what information students have mastered, as well as what content or skills need to be retaught. This type of diagnosis can be very valuable to teachers. Unfortunately, too few instructors use tests in this way. Because of the pressure of time and the need to "cover" the content, it is more likely that teachers will test and quickly move on to the next lessons. Still, there are many teachers who do use tests to ensure that all of their students are prepared to move on.

Historically, test results have also been used as a way of arriving at grades. Although a student's final grade in a class often includes evaluations of homework assignments, projects, and sometimes oral presentations, test results have often been the primary factor in a teacher's decision on a report card grade. These report card grades have traditionally been the determining factor on whether a student is promoted to the next level or is given a high school diploma. In most states, tests have been devised by the individual teacher of the class or, perhaps in larger schools, on a departmental level. For example, a group of three of four teachers who all teach eleventh-grade English might develop a final examination for their school. With the exception of New York State, which has long had statewide examinations at the high school level, most tests were prepared and graded in individual school buildings. The Regents examinations in New York State have always been developed at the state level, and although they are graded by individual teachers, each year several of the examinations given in the state are called to Albany (the state capital) for regrading. Even in New York, students in the past have been able to move to the next grade level or graduate from high school without passing these high-stakes tests. A student failing a Regents examination could receive a passing grade for the course if his or her grades for the four quarters were high enough. The Regents grade was only counted as one fifth of the final course grade. It was also true that only approximately 50 percent of New York State students were taking the Regents exams. An easier non-Regents test was available for those students who chose not to challenge the more difficult exam.

With the onset of high-stakes testing, New York State, like many other states, has increased its requirements for high school graduation. Initially, the state board of education, known as the Board of Regents, established a goal that all New York State students must pass the required Regents tests in order to receive a high school diploma. This change was to be gradually implemented over a period of years. During the transition, the passing grade on Regents examinations was set at 55 percent rather than the traditional 65 percent. As in other states, the goal of having all students pass the high-stakes test resulted in controversy concerning the expectations for disabled and bilingual students. There were also concerns that this new requirement would lead to increased high school dropouts as students became discouraged or frustrated in their efforts to pass the tests. Although the passing grade for Regents examinations was scheduled to be raised to 65 percent in 2003, the Board of Regents voted to allow districts to continue to use 55 percent as the passing score. As a compromise measure, New York State has also introduced several levels of diplomas depending on students' scores on the tests. In addition, accommodations have been developed for students with serious learning problems.

Even in states such as New York where tests have been important, their significance has increased both for students and professional staff. The biggest change has been the practice of using test results not only to measure how students are learning, but also utilizing them to hold schools accountable. This new accountability has also introduced measures to punish schools that fail to improve students' scores. Under the current provisions of national legislation, parents of students in schools that fail to meet minimum test score standards will have the right to have their children attend a different public school. As a result, it is possible that in the future a failing school would lose enough students that it would be unable to continue to operate.

Proponents of this type of accountability point to what they see as a long history of failing schools in the United States. It is primarily the test scores from such schools that have resulted in the poor showing of American students in comparison with students in other countries. The feeling of the critics, as articulated in the *A Nation at Risk* and other reports, is that our public schools have been allowed to experiment with electives and untested teaching techniques, and that they have not been held accountable to perform their primary function, which is to teach basic academic content and skills. This critique of our schools goes on to argue that other organizations in our society need to have standards and be accountable, and the same must be true with our schools. Society must determine what children need to know and be able to do (standards) and then assure that these standards are being met using high-stakes tests and school accountability reports. It has been this approach that has dominated the reform movement during the past two decades.

Unlike the strategy of establishing statewide curriculum standards, the practice of mandating high-stakes testing has resulted in significant opposition from both educators and some parents. For Scott Thompson, in an article published in the *Phi Delta Kappan*, which was later published in the *Education Digest*, high-stakes testing is "the Evil Twin of Authentic Standards." For this author and many others,

authentic, standards-based reform is fundamentally concerned with equity. It departs radically from the tracking and sorting carried out by the factory-style school of yore. Instead, it aims to hold high expectations and *provide high levels of support* for all students, teachers, and educational leaders.

Under the evil twins' version of standards and accountability, we see students retained in grade because of a single test score, and we typically see a corresponding increase in dropout rates where such *worst* practice is in place. Equity then becomes the casualty rather than the fruit of reform. And as Sandra Feldman, president of the American Federation of Teachers, recently observed, "when tests become the be-all and end-all, they deform, not reform, education. . . ."

What gets lost when teachers and students are pressured to make students better test-takers is precisely the rich, high-level teaching and learning that authentic, standards-based reform aims to promote in all classrooms and for all students.[1]

One of the cautions raised by those who question an overemphasis on tests is that under no circumstance should an educational decision be made solely or automatically as a result of a single test. In Massachusetts, where passing state tests was made mandatory for high school graduation, parents and students held demonstrations and petitioned the legislature to change the policy.

A number of states have had situations where teachers and administrators have been found guilty of cheating in an attempt to ensure that students receive passing grades. A school district in Houston, Texas, is now being investigated for improper practices in reporting test results. In New York State, the scores in both a math Regents and the physics Regents had to be changed because the tests were deemed to be unfair. Testing experts also point to the unfairness of establishing a specific cutoff point for determining a passing score. They point out that, like opinion polls, test results have a "standard margin of error."

Others question the underlying premises of high-stakes testing and accountability. "Neo-conservative reformers" seem to believe that "American schools are failing because students, teachers, and other educators are confused or because they lack the ability or will to engage in focused education." In order to improve schools, these individuals claim that students and educators need to be motivated to work harder. High-stakes tests will provide the necessary motivation for improving on the status quo. For some critics, testing is a type of "intrinsic sanction" and is a poor strategy for improving student learning. In a book entitled *The Manufactured Crisis*, David Berliner and Bruce Biddle have written that society should "consider, first, the problem for students." Psychologists have written that when students are merely forced to memorize content they will not succeed in understanding concepts nor will they develop the capacity for creative thinking.[2]

The same authors argue that the competition inherent in high-stakes testing and accountability is unfair. Many critics have pointed out that such competition is not being played on "a level playing field." In releasing data, some states have included comparisons of test results among schools with similar characteristics, but in all states, state and county averages are likely to be published. The wealth or poverty of families in the district, along with the level of financial support available to a school, can affect test results. In some places including California, wealthy suburban districts have received financial bonuses for outstanding test scores. Even the practice of emphasizing "gains" in scores can be affected by many factors that are beyond the control of educators in a school district.[3] An influx of children with disabilities or Limited English Proficiency can affect the test results of a school or grade level, especially in small schools. Low salaries can result in high teacher turnover and the loss of outstanding teachers. Such turnover is one of the major problems in many rural and urban schools. Too often, experienced and able teachers are tempted by higher salaries and improved working conditions and choose to leave schools where they are needed.

One of the most often repeated criticisms of high-stakes testing is that it leads to significant stress on teachers and students. In a book entitled *Crisis in Education: Stress and Burnout in the American Teacher*, Barry Farber writes that some teachers have the

> feeling that society expects them to educate, socialize, and graduate virtually every student who comes to school, regardless of the social, economic, familial, or psychological difficulties some of these students bring with them. Even if parents, psychologists, social workers, and various public and private helping agencies have failed, teachers are still expected to succeed and will be held accountable if they do not. For many teachers, the public cry for accountability is no more than a new, more sophisticated way of expecting schools and teachers to cure all the ills of society.[4]

Teachers talk of sleepless nights as they worry about the big exams. Despite the fact that a teacher might have more students with learning difficulties than other faculty members teaching the same course, most schools do not take this into account when test results are published. Competition within a grade level for the best test results may not be talked about, but it is certainly on teachers' minds. A third-grade teacher faced with a high-stakes test can also be very critical of colleagues who taught the children at the lower grades. In reality, the third-grade test really is assessing what the students learned in kindergarten, first, and second grade, as well as third grade. Even though this is the case, it is the teacher at the grade level where the test is given who assumes most of the stress and pressure. Some principals, feeling that they are being judged by test results, will put pressure on teachers. This additional stress is felt most by principals or teachers who have yet to achieve tenure in the district. Other principals and superintendents who are engaged in attempting to build a positive resume seek to do so by improving the test scores in his or her school. A school administrator who can point to improved scores is likely to be a prime candidate for a leadership position in another district seeking to upgrade student achievement.

In states such as South Carolina, Indiana, and Kentucky, teachers and schools are being motivated to improve scores by financial rewards. The reward program in South Carolina gives to "the top 25 percent of schools in each of 5 socioeconomic categories" awards ranging from ten thousand to seventy thousand dollars for improving their test scores. It is also true that states and school systems are factoring "students' standardized test scores into their decisions to hire, fire, and promote teachers." In St. Louis, these scores are a category on the teacher evaluation forms. If a faculty member receives an unsatisfactory rating in this category, their salary could be frozen, or they could face dismissal if there is "no improvement in the scores within 100 days."[5]

Although students and parents have organized to protest and even boycott tests, such tactics are much more difficult for teachers. In this regard, Alfie Kohn, a well-known educator, noted in his book *The Schools Our Children Deserve* that in other countries teachers have protested examinations that were imposed by the government. Japanese teachers, "through their collective refusal to administer" tests to elementary children, were able to end the practice. "In 1993, teachers in England and Wales basically stopped the new national testing program in its tracks, at least for a while, by a similar act of civil disobedience."[6]

Teachers and administrators are not the only ones who could feel significant stress because of high-stakes testing. There are many educators and parents who are worried about the additional pressure on the students. With the passage of the No Child Left Behind Act, mandatory testing will be required each year for all students in grades three through eight. Some parents have reported that their children have demonstrated extreme anxiety over testing which caused some students to become physically ill. The fear of failing to graduate from high school with one's own class could create serious psychological problems for high school seniors. Of course there is also the concern that such students would choose to drop out of school altogether. In addition, there are students who talk about and believe that they just do not "test well." These students will claim, "I knew the stuff when I went in the room but went blank when I tried to answer the questions."

Perhaps one of the most common criticisms of a heavy reliance on tests as the major method of assessing student work is the concern about the practice known as "teaching to the test." The overriding importance of tests puts pressure on teachers to use class time only to deal with topics that are likely to appear on the examination. As a result, class discussions on other related topics of interest for students are curtailed. Using teaching techniques such as cooperative or group learning, projects, or even field trips are limited because of the need to "cover the content." Teachers complain that the learning activities that students enjoy and benefit from the most are often omitted because they take time away from making sure students are ready to take the tests. Weeks and sometimes more than a month are saved at the end of the course for extensive review and practice taking sample tests. Just as students take courses on test taking for the Scholastic Assessment Test required by colleges, test-taking techniques and tips are a part of many school programs.

It is not likely that protests by students, parents, or teachers will, in the near future, end the reliance on high-stakes testing. On the other hand, many critics of high-stakes testing will continue to protest what they feel is a misguided educational practice. Unfortunately, some of these critics have been slow to offer suggestions for alternative methods of assessment. Typically, the critics of traditional testing are most vehement about the validity of objective or short-answer questions. Although true-and-false or fill-in-the-blank questions have become less frequently used, the multiple-choice type question remains popular.

Especially in courses other than math and science, assessment experts urge teachers to use essay questions. One widely discussed model in a book entitled *Assessing Student Outcomes* was published by the respected Association for Supervision and Curriculum Development. Called the *Dimensions of Learning*, it is an instructional and assessment model that is dependent on "five types of thinking" that "are essential to the learning process." They include the following:

- Dimension 1: Positive Attitudes and Perception About Learning
- Dimension 2: Acquiring and Integrating Knowledge
- Dimension 3: Extending and Refining Knowledge
- Dimension 4: Using Knowledge Meaningfully
- Dimension 5: Productive Habits of Mind

To measure student progress in each of these areas, rubrics have been prepared. The "rubric consists of four levels of performance for each given standard, each of which is assigned a score ranging from a low of one to a high of four." The authors have included numerous rubrics for both teachers and students that can be adapted for use in the classroom.[7]

Assessments such as the one mentioned above are much more sophisticated and difficult to implement than merely giving students multiple-choice tests. Educators have introduced a number of alternatives to the traditional test and have even found ways within an examination to assess student skills as well as knowledge. As part of the New York State earth science Regents, students are required to complete a "hands-on" exercise that seeks to measure laboratory skills. The foreign language exam now includes a portion of the test devoted to assessing students' ability to speak the language. In social studies, students are asked document-based questions to assess their ability to interpret historical sources, political cartoons, and graphs or charts. Needless to say, there have to be well-thought-out rubrics to assist teachers in assigning credit for sections of examinations that utilize these types of assessments.

The portfolio represents another tool for judging a student's academic progress. In the state of Vermont, portfolios are required for all students as a graduation requirement. The purpose is to provide a record of a student's work and to allow teachers to trace a student's progress by examining samples of assignments completed as part of classroom activities. Portfolios have long been required for art students, and in a number of districts they have been mandated in English. Other schools are now requiring that seniors complete a project, which includes a major paper along with an oral presentation. Like the use of portfolios, such projects or presentations have been made a requirement for graduation.

As a result of the growing doubts about the validity of using only high-stakes testing to measure student academic achievement, the various types of alternative assessment have been given the label "authentic assessment." This term is given to the use of portfolios and performance-based tasks. Supporters believe that they "present a broader, more genuine picture of student learning."[8] For advocates of authentic assessment, the approach will more effectively nurture "complex understandings," develop "reflective habits of mind," document "students' evolving understandings," and make "use of assessment as a moment of learning. . . . If assessment is to be a moment in an educational process rather than simply an evaluative vehicle, then it must be seen and used as an opportunity to develop complex understandings."[9]

Supporters of standardized testing often have reservations about the validity of those techniques being suggested by the proponents of authentic assessment. It can be argued that tests provide educators with information that other forms of assessment cannot. For instance, tests can:

- Provide information that is more standardized and consistent from school to school or district to district than the results of measures based on an individual teacher's judgment
- Be used to compare achievement across different classrooms, schools, or districts, or between various racial, ethnic, income, and other subgroups of students
- Provide valuable summary information about student performance by subject, skill, and knowledge area
- Be collected, analyzed, and reported efficiently at a relatively low cost[10]

Even if schools were to develop a more varied system of high-stakes assessments, there would still be concerns about requiring every student to meet higher academic standards. Two groups in particular are cited as being most at risk. Approximately 11 percent of our nation's students have been identified as being eligible for special education services. Such learning problems would range from students who have visual, hearing, and physical disabilities, to a student who might have a high IQ but has a speech impediment. If all students are going to be required to pass a test or meet some other assessment criteria in order to receive a high school diploma, what sort of accommodations should be made for special education students? This is a serious question for state education agencies and for individual schools. Increasingly we have a growing number of students identified as having Limited English Proficiency. It must be determined whether these students will be given special consideration such as taking tests in their native language.

In any case most observers would agree that merely requiring high-stakes testing, even with carefully planned learning standards, will not in itself bring about a significant growth in student learning. It is difficult to disagree with the words of Richard Elmore when he wrote in *Harvard Magazine* that "test-based accountability without substantial investments in internal accountability and instructional improvement is unlikely to elicit better performance from low-performing students and schools." Not everyone but many would support his contention that

> The increased pressure of test-based accountability alone is likely to *aggravate* the existing inequalities between low-performing and high-performing schools and students. Most high-performing schools simply reflect the social capital of their students (they are primarily schools with students of high socioeconomic status), rather than the internal capacity of schools themselves. Most low-performing schools cannot rely on the social capital of students and families and instead must rely on their organizational capacity. With little or no investment in capacity, low-performing schools get worse relative to high-performing schools.[11]

Whether it be a high or low-performing school, it will be the individual teachers in the classroom who will most affect the success of educational reform. The *A Nation at Risk* report recognized the importance of improving the teaching profession, and it is to this initiative that we now turn.

NOTES

1. Scott Thompson, "The Evil Twin of 'Authentic Standards,'" *Education Digest* 66, no. 8 (April 2001): 13.

2. Davis C. Berliner and Bruce J. Biddle, *The Manufactured Crisis* (Reading, MA: Addison-Wesley Publishing, 1995), 191–92.

3. Berliner and Biddle, *The Manufactured Crisis*, 199.

4. Barry A. Farber, *Crisis in Education: Stress and Burnout in the American Teacher* (San Francisco: Jossey-Bass Publishers, 1991), 61.

5. Thomas Toch, *In the Name of Excellence* (New York: Oxford University Press, 1991), 206–207.

6. Alfie Kohn, *The Schools Our Children Deserve* (Boston: Houghton Mifflin Company, 1999), 207–208.

7. Robert J. Marzano, Debra Pickering, and Jay McTighe, *Assessing Student Outcomes* (Alexandria, VA: Association For Supervision and Curriculum Development, 1993), 1–3, V.

8. Vito Perrone, ed., *Expanding Student Assessment* (Alexandria, VA: Association For Supervision and Curriculum Development, 1991), 49.

9. Perrone, *Expanding Student Assessment*, 51.

10. Nancy Kober, "What Tests Can and Cannot Tell Us," *Test Talk For Leaders*, October 2002, www.cep-dc.org/testing/testtalkoctober2002.htm (accessed 7 December 2003).

11. Richard R. Elmore, "Testing Trap," *Harvard Magazine*, September–October 2002, www.harvard-magazine.com/on-line/0902140.html (accessed 7 December 2003).

CHAPTER 8

The Teachers

The Findings section of the *A Nation at Risk* report states "that not enough of the academically able students are being attracted to teaching; that teacher preparation programs need substantial improvement; that the professional working life of teachers is on the whole unacceptable; and that a serious shortage of teachers exists in key fields."[1] Many of the other studies released during the 1980s pointed to similar deficiencies (see chapter 4). To remedy these problems, the authors of *A Nation at Risk* made seven recommendations. To assess the effect of these suggestions, we need to consider how each has been dealt with during the past two decades.

The first of the seven deals with preparing more competent teachers by improving our teacher education programs. In this regard, many efforts have been made in recent years. Although the National Teacher Examination (NTE) was initiated in 1940 by the National Council on Education, it was not widely used to judge applicants for teacher certification until after 1985. Achieving a satisfactory score on this examination is now required by thirty states. There are three separate types of tests offered, and not all of them are used by every state:

The *Praxis I: Preprofessional Skills Test* consists of hour-long academic skills tests in reading, writing, and mathematics. These basic tests apply to prospective teachers in all fields and all grades, and are required in thirty states for admission into teacher education, or to obtain an initial teaching license.

The *Praxis II* assesses subject area, pedagogy, and professional educational knowledge, offering more than 140 exams in subjects ranging from art to social studies.

The *Praxis III* is a classroom performance assessment of teaching skills, covering classroom management, instructional planning, and assessment of student learning.[2]

Despite the existence of these examinations, the passing score accepted on the NTE examination varies from state to state. While a majority of the states use this examination, some states such as New York have developed their own examination and have recently raised the passing scores required for certification. The result in New York has been to further restrict the number of teachers accepted for certification.

As with every effort to improve education, there are critics of the idea of using examinations to select teachers. Some have suggested that these tests are "incredibly easy" and that they do not measure classroom competence. Others question whether one's ability to teach can be measured by a test, and they point to the fact that there is "a lack of evidence supporting the idea that teacher testing predicts teacher performance."[3]

Supporters say that at a minimum, the test can determine something about the literacy level of the candidate and also measure to some degree the content understanding. With so many teachers lacking a major in an academic discipline, the test can give an indication of whether the prospective teacher has some basic understanding of the subject that he or she wishes to teach. In addition, education methods tests can at least find out if the candidate has been exposed to a variety of teaching and classroom management techniques. In any case, almost every state has used these tests to eliminate individuals from entering the public school classroom as certified teachers.

Certification standards have been raised in other ways. Although a bachelor's degree has been a requirement for many years, the necessity of acquiring a master's degree to achieve any type of permanent certification is increasingly being required in a number of states. In other states, it is being studied as a possible requirement. In New York State, the Board of Regents during the late 1990s seriously considered requiring that a teacher have a master's degree before receiving any type of certification. Because of pressure from administrators and boards of education, a compromise was reached. Beginning in 2004, New York State teachers will be granted Initial Certification with a bachelor's degree but will only receive professional certification if, within three years, they earn an appropriate master's degree while at the same time gaining three years of teaching experience in their field of certification. This new requirement is likely to lead many potential teachers in the United States to go directly to full-time graduate study after receiving their four-year degree. Needless to say there are many educators in the state who feel that the three-year window is much too restrictive, especially when considering that the teacher must also have three years of full-time teaching experience during the same period. New York has also eliminated the practice of permanent certification. Those certified beginning in 2004 must participate in ongoing staff development requirements in order to maintain their certification. Similar to other professions, such as medicine and accounting, teachers will be required to continue to update their skills. Other states also have adopted this approach. Although school bus drivers had been required to undergo fingerprint screening for many years, in New York State, at least, no such process was in place for future teachers. Currently, anyone working in a New York public school must undergo fingerprint screening. New York also requires training in child abuse and prevention of student violence. In a unique effort to judge a candidate's ability to teach effectively, a videotaped lesson must also be submitted to the state education department to achieve professional certification.

Other states have instituted similar programs to raise the standards for achieving certification. However, those teaching in private schools do not have to have certification. Charter schools, which are paid for with public money, in many places have significant latitude in hiring noncertified teachers. It is also true that those parents who homeschool their children are not required to be certified. Even with higher standards for certification, or perhaps because of them, there are still many people teaching in our public schools without appropriate certification. The *A Nation at Risk* report noted in 1983 that

- Despite widespread publicity about an overpopulation of teachers, severe shortages of certain kinds of teachers exist in the fields of mathematics, science, and foreign languages; and among special-

ists in education for gifted and talented, language minority, and handicapped students.
- The shortage of teachers in mathematics and science is particularly severe. A 1981 survey of forty-five states revealed shortages of mathematics teachers in forty-three states, critical shortages of earth science teachers in thirty-three states, and of physics teachers everywhere.
- Half of the newly employed mathematics, science, and English teachers are not qualified to teach these subjects; fewer than one-third of U.S. high schools offer physics taught by qualified teachers.[4]

There is little question that lack of proper certification is still prevalent in many areas in the United States. A study in 1996 reported that more than 50,000 people who lack appropriate training enter the profession annually. These individuals most often are issued "emergency" licenses. "These numbers have only increased since then. One recent study in California suggests that half of all first year teachers do not have their credentials when they begin teaching."[5] Because of the inability to staff our classrooms with certified teachers, it has become necessary throughout the country to find shortcuts in the certification process.

In a 2002 report, "Meeting the Highly Qualified Teacher Challenge," the U.S. Secretary of Education essentially calls for the abolition of professional education as it currently exists. The report concludes that states should cease requiring traditional teacher education. Instead, "states will need to streamline their certification system to focus on the few things that really matter: verbal ability, content knowledge, and, as a safety precaution, a background check of new teachers."[6]

This report and other critics of the current method for preparing teachers have charged that there is an overemphasis on methods classes and that there is too little attention paid to academic content courses. For Pam Grossman, writing in the *Harvard Education Letter*, this emphasis on content preparation ignores "research indicating the courses in how to teach a subject contribute more to a teacher's success than additional subject-matter courses."[7]

Whether or not one agrees with the current standards for certification or not, these requirements are not likely to change dramatically in the near future. Those areas lacking state certified teachers are located primarily in our major cities and in rural areas. They are also found most often in the subject areas identified in the *A Nation at Risk* report. For example, a 2003 study discovered that, particularly in ten states, there were significant problems. In the United States, 14.9 percent of the classes in English were being taught by uncertified teachers; in Mississippi, the percentage was 23.6. In mathematics nationwide, 17.8 percent of the classes were being taught by those who had not met certification requirements, while in Mississippi, Kentucky, and Louisiana, the percentage is over 20 percent. The science classes in Kentucky have 20.1 percent of their teachers not meeting state requirements, while the national average in science is 12.5 percent. In New York State, the Board of Regents has placed a time limit for districts to achieve a 100 percent certification rate for all teachers. Currently, accomplishing this ambitious goal seems to be far off.

Another concern is the tendency to hire "out of field" teachers at the middle school level. A national study during the 1999–2000 school year showed that this tendency was obvious in the fields of English, math, science, and social studies.[8] The practice of hiring less qualified teachers at the middle school level is occurring despite the fact that our nation's standardized test scores are often lowest during this period of a student's education.

The current efforts of states to raise teacher certification requirements have been extensive, and although it is difficult to gauge the effect on student learning, it remains a significant initiative in creating a more selective and better-prepared teaching profession. Perhaps one of the most promising developments in elevating the profession can be found in the effort to create a truly national certification. In 1986,

The Carnegie Task Force on Teaching as a Profession, in its pivotal report, *A Nation Prepared: Teachers for the 21st Century*, called for the establishment of a National Board for Professional Teaching Standards. The following year this unique institution in the life of American education was born.

The National Board's mission is to advance the quality of teaching and learning by:

- maintaining high and rigorous standards for what accomplished teachers should know and be able to do,
- providing a national voluntary system certifying teachers who meet these standards and

- advocating related education reforms to integrate National Board Certification in American education and to capitalize on the expertise of National Board Certified Teachers.[9]

By 2002, 16,044 teachers throughout the nation had attained National Board Certification. Many school districts have established incentives for their teachers by providing salary bonuses for those instructors who meet the National Board's standards. In addition, these teachers can more easily move from state to state, as most states will grant automatic certification based on the achievement of national certification.

To become board certified, a teacher must "complete a series of performance-based assessments, including written exercises that reflect a mastery of their subject and understanding of the most effective teaching methods." Also, they must supply samples of students' work, videotapes of their teaching, be interviewed, and take part in simulations at special assessment centers.[10]

This new certification method is also helping to achieve another recommendation of the *A Nation at Risk* report. In creating a highly respected honor for experienced teachers, which in many cases has resulted in additional compensation, national certification succeeds in providing a "career ladder" for the profession that works to "distinguish among the beginning instructor, the experienced teacher, and the master teacher."[11] Even the supporters of the National Board Certification program would not claim that it alone will raise the effectiveness of teachers throughout the nation, as only a small number of teachers have thus far chosen to participate. On the other hand, there are many who believe that it

> can be a catalyst for lasting change. It can redefine teaching as a career by stimulating new incentive structures, staffing patterns and organizational arrangements. . . . Most importantly, as these related changes both increase the flow of first-rate people in the field and stem the tide of those departing, and as teachers' roles and responsibilities are more sensibly structured, National Board Certification can become a pathway to improved student learning.[12]

It is certainly true that certification programs for teachers have become an important method being used to upgrade the profession. For the Commission on Excellence, which prepared the *A Nation at Risk* report, the programs that trained teachers in the early 1980s were not effective. As noted earlier, the Commission's findings highlighted an overemphasis on "educational methods" classes. In their recommendations, they suggested that colleges and universities offering teacher education programs "be judged by how well their graduates demonstrated an aptitude for teaching" and "competence in an academic discipline."[13] At least in part because of the attention caused by the *A Nation at Risk* report, state governments have focused on improving programs that prepare teachers. Formal accreditation of these programs has been a primary vehicle for ensuring their quality. For many years, college teacher education programs have been accredited either by the national agency known as the National Council for the Accreditation of Teacher Education (NCATE) or more likely by a state education department. NCATE accreditation is a demanding process for any college teacher education department. It requires producing comprehensive descriptions of the program, specific assessment measures, and ends with a visitation to the campus by a team of experts. Because it is a very time-consuming process for college faculty and administrators, a majority of the teacher education programs have not sought national accreditation.

Dissatisfaction with the process has led in recent years to the formation of a new accreditation agency known as Teacher Education Accreditation Council (TEAC) which will compete with NCATE. In 2003, the federal Department of Education approved TEAC, and the new organization has begun accrediting teacher education programs throughout the nation. In an attempt to improve programs in New York State, the Board of Regents has mandated that each college in the state be reaccredited by 2006. As part of this process, every program had to gain approval of the State Education Department to ensure that its curriculums conformed to new state guidelines. Among the guidelines was a reemphasis on academic content even for prospective elementary teachers. Perhaps the most far-reaching and helpful new requirement was to mandate that teacher education students have significant experience in an elementary or secondary classroom prior to their semester of student teaching. A student seeking to be dually certified as an elementary and special education teacher would be required to have a minimum of 150 hours of classroom observation and participation. At least some of this work has to be in a "high needs" district, which are most often located in an urban area.

Other states also have revamped their teacher education programs, most often tying them with the specific education curriculum standards adopted in their state. Such reforms along with renewed pressure for accreditation have created within the colleges of education the need to engage in introspection and to rewrite many of their programs. There is reason to believe that these initiatives will have positive results. If nothing else, the teacher education programs, which have often been labeled as "cash cows" for institutions of higher education, are now receiving more attention. In most cases, this could mean increased budgets, improvements to the library, revamping facilities, and even hiring new faculty.

Higher academic standards within these programs might also be causing teacher education departments to raise their admission standards. Some institutions have used state certification examinations as a way to screen candidates before they are allowed to student teach. Other programs have required minimum grade point averages for students wishing to take advanced courses in the teacher education program. Colleges and universities cannot afford to graduate students in teacher education who cannot pass the state certification examinations. Passing rates for students in specific colleges are even made public in some states. A college with a high passing rate can use it as a factor for drawing new students into their program.

There are several indicators that would suggest that teacher education programs are improving. In an annual survey in which teachers evaluate their preparation programs, 64 percent of those surveyed in 1997 gave either an A or a B grade to their college program. In 1984, the percentage giving an A or a B was 49 percent. Those students assigning a D or an F grade dropped by 38 percent during the same time period. By 1997, 90 percent of teachers gave their college training a grade of C or better.[14]

Another somewhat encouraging indicator is performance on the Adult Prose Literacy Test. Although scientists, lawyers, and judges scored highest, teachers' scores were comparable to physicians, writers, and social workers.[15] It can only be helpful that society has become somewhat more selective in choosing who enters the profession, as there is little doubt that well-prepared and motivated teachers make a difference.

[A] study of high- and low-achieving schools with similar student populations in New York City found that differences in teacher qualifications accounted for more than 90 percent of the variation in student achievement in reading and mathematics at all grade levels tested. Research using national data and studies in Georgia, Michigan, and Virginia have found that students achieve at higher levels and are less likely to drop out when they are taught by teachers with certification in their teaching field, by those with master's degrees and by teachers enrolled in graduate studies.[16]

Along with improved preparation for teachers, the *A Nation at Risk* report called for increased teacher salaries, which would be "professionally competitive, market sensitive, and performance based."[17] Pam Grossman has summarized the trend in teacher salaries as follows:

While there has been some progress in raising teaching salaries over the past two decades, by and large teacher salaries nationwide have not kept up with inflation. A recent report by the National Center for Education Statistics found that, after adjusting for inflation, teachers' salaries actually declined 1 percent between 1990–1991 and 2000–2001.[18]

In the same essay, Grossman includes John Goodlad's explanation for the lack of progress. It was Goodlad's opinion that shortages in teachers, which might have increased wages, were reduced by the practice of many states of granting temporary and emergency certificates. These certificates were easy to obtain and in many areas caused a "glut of teachers."[19] Other surveys also show that in comparison with other professions, both the average starting salary and the average salary of all teachers remains quite low. One survey in the year 2000 gave as an average annual starting salary of all teachers, the figure $27,989, while a liberal arts major began at $36,201. The starting salaries of all other professions surveyed were significantly higher than teachers. With average salaries in other professional positions, the gap was even larger.[20] Another study done by the American Federation of Teachers purports that in the year 2000, on average, "teachers' relative standard of living is the lowest in forty years."[21]

At the same time that average salary figures are low, it must be pointed out that salary schedules for teachers vary greatly. Starting and average salaries in different states clearly show that one's salary depends on where one teaches. For the 1999–2000 school year for instance, Connecticut had an average annual salary for teachers of $52,410, while in South Dakota the average was $29,072. New York State had the highest average beginning annual salary of $31,910, while North Dakota teachers began their career with an average salary of $20,422.[22] As noted earlier, the difference within states is also very dramatic, with property-rich suburban areas paying significantly higher salaries than poor rural or urban districts. From all of these figures, one can only conclude that as a nation, we have paid little attention to the recommendation in the *A Nation at Risk* report to raise teacher salaries.

While it might be argued that these salaries have been "market sensitive," they have not in most places become "performance based." It is also true that the recommendations to create some type of "merit pay" for teachers has not been followed in most districts. Although the idea has been discussed for many decades, and there have been successful experiments in a number of school districts, the idea most often has been opposed by teachers' unions.

The primary concern has been a reluctance to agree upon an acceptable evaluation process. At least in the minds of many teachers, such a process is much more complicated than in many other occupations. Teachers worry about any system which is based primarily on evaluations done by school administrators who may or may not be well qualified to judge a teacher's work. While an administrator might have expertise in one academic field, he or she may not be able to judge fairly the work of a physics teacher or a faculty member teaching a foreign language that the principal does not speak. Other teachers view what they do as more of an art than a science and do not wish to have their compensation based on the judgment of a principal or a department head whose view of teaching techniques might be very narrow. Consideration of student reviews of faculty members is also unacceptable to many teachers. Even older students can be swayed by the grades they receive or by other factors having little to do with a teachers' competence. Having peers rate a colleague's performance is viewed by some as a potential disruption to the collegial atmosphere of a school. The current suggestion that compensation somehow be tied to student test scores is feared even more by many teachers. Thus, the most typical type of compensation method used by school districts remains a set salary schedule based on years of experience. Most districts offer additional salary for a master's degree and possibly for graduate credit beyond a master's. Although the number of experiments taking place using "performance based" salary plans may have increased slightly during the past two decades, this approach remains an exception to the norm.

The *A Nation at Risk* report links compensation, tenure, and retention decisions to an "effective evaluation system that includes peer review."[23] Peer review systems have been put in place in Minneapolis, Cincinnati, and Columbus, Ohio.[24] Teachers' unions in various districts are considering peer review as a practice, but taking the next step of linking this process with salary is occurring more slowly. The fact is that any change in either the method of compensation or evaluation of teachers is most often an issue dealt with during the collective bargaining process. As a result, school districts are not in a position to impose new systems on unwilling faculties. Thus, it is quite clear that during the past twenty years most evaluations of teachers continue to be done by principals or other district administrators.

There also has been little activity in implementing the recommendation that "school boards should adopt an eleven-month contract for teachers. This would ensure time for curriculum and professional development, programs for students with special needs, and a more adequate level of teacher compensation."[25] While high-stakes testing has caused some districts to establish additional summer programs for students who have fallen behind, teachers choosing to work in the summer have most often been paid a summer school wage rather than being given an eleven-month contract. It is true that many districts do pay teachers for curriculum work during the summer, but this too is most often paid for on a daily or weekly basis. Adding a full month's salary to a teacher's contract would be an extremely expensive option for most districts, and in most communities it has never been considered.

While the idea of eleven-month contracts has not caught on, the idea of "career ladders" for teachers has become more popular. Designed to reward outstanding professionals, many districts have devised ways to reward effective faculty members.

A 1996 report by the National Commission for Teaching and America's Future said creating new career paths for teachers—sometimes called "master teacher" or "leader teacher" programs—is one of the best ways to give leading educators the respect they deserve and ensure their methods spread quickly and broadly.[26]

The seventy-nine schools currently being operated by the company known as Edison Schools have adopted a lead-teacher system that uses "accomplished classroom teachers to advise other instructors at their grade level." Depending on the situation, these lead-teachers can earn up to an additional $10,000 for their mentoring duties. An interesting experiment in five public schools in Arizona, funded by the Milken Family Foundation, has the goal of a $100,000 annual salary for their outstanding teachers who are acting as mentors.[27]

The most popular approach to the career ladder concept has been creating positions for mentor teachers. Along with offering extra compensation as part of such a program, mentors can help to stem the attrition of new teachers leaving the district. Mentors can offer non-threatening assistance in areas such as teaching methods and classroom management. They can also be helpful in assisting a new teacher to adjust to the social aspects of the school and community. Most programs attempt to separate mentors from the formal evaluation process so that a new teacher can feel comfortable sharing his or her concerns. Many mentor plans are developed with the cooperation of the teachers' union, and release time and additional compensation are negotiated as part of the contract.

A more sophisticated career ladder plan might include three or more classifications such as the college system of naming instructors: assistant professors, associate professors, and full professors. Although the titles used would be different, some public schools have also based salaries on a teacher's rank within such a system. With the exception of establishing mentor programs, the career ladder approach urged in the *A Nation at Risk* report has not been widely implemented.

A number of states have also paid some attention to the recommendation that practicing teachers participate in "designing teacher education programs." This was also a recommendation of the *A Nation at Risk* report.[28] Such involvement occurred at both the state level and at individual colleges. During the preparation of revised state mandates and of curriculum standards, state government officials have frequently held public hearings open to teachers or have sought input from committees including classroom teachers. Teacher education programs in colleges and universities are also encouraged or even mandated by their state to establish advisory committees that include teachers. Especially at the state level, teachers' unions have sought to be part of any changes that affect the preparation of new teachers. Very often unions do support upgrading requirements for new teachers but are careful about agreeing to any additional mandates for their current membership.

Certainly one of the more controversial recommendations in the Teacher section of the *A Nation at Risk* report was the suggestion that encouraged the development of alternate ways for preparing college graduates to quickly meet the demand for new teachers. Such programs are most likely to be developed in fields such as math and science education. The *A Nation at Risk* report specifically suggests that "recent college graduates with math and science degrees, graduate students, and industrial and retired scientists," be allowed to be rapidly trained and begin almost immediately teaching in our schools.[29]

The most widely known initiative of this type is in the program entitled Teach for America (TFA). Begun in 1990, the program has already produced 7,500 teachers. Currently, "3,100 corps members are reaching 260,000 students" throughout the nation.[30] Teach for America is a nonprofit organization that attempts to recruit academically talented college students who will agree to teach for two years in "high need" schools which are located primarily in urban and rural communities. Recruits receive five weeks of intensive training during the summer, including some student teaching. Once they begin teaching in the fall, they attend weekly professional development workshops. They must also meet any state requirement for alternative teacher education programs. This might mean a requirement that they also enroll in graduate programs or attend school district seminars for uncertified teachers. Although it is impossible to provide conclusive evidence of the overall effectiveness of the program, supporters would point to an article published in April of 2001 in a publication called *Education Next* which stated that "it's becoming clear that Teach for America is channeling a wealth of talent, energy, and activity into educational leadership that might otherwise have wound up in such fields as medicine, law, or business."[31] An individual study done by the Houston public school system demonstrated a positive success rate for those teachers in the TFA program. When they were compared with all teachers in the district, the TFA teachers performed just as well, if not better, than the total pool of teachers. Of course it is true that many of the teachers in the pool were also not certified in their field.[32]

Detractors are quick to point out that despite their idealism and enthusiasm, these fledgling teachers lack the necessary "pedagogical training and knowledge of child development theories." It is for some "a Peace Corps–style rescue mission rather than a true profession, with salaries appropriate to attracting solid candidates." Linda Darling-Hammond has written about the program and has charged that "TFA has recruiters and advocates who have focused much of their attention on the advantaged college graduates for whom TFA serves as something useful to do on their way to their 'real jobs' in law, medicine, or business."[33] She and others have criticized the "quickie" licenses given to these and other teachers prepared in alternate teacher education programs.[34] Critics point out that only one-third of the participants in the program stay in teaching after their two-year contract ends. Defenders counter with the statistic that 45 to 50 percent of all teachers leave the profession after two years.[35]

Politically, Teach for America has become a source of heated debate. As part of the AmeriCorps program, it is dependent on budget decisions made by the officials of AmeriCorps. Each participant in Teach for America receives $4,725 per year in scholarship money. Despite President Bush's apparent support for Teach for America, his administration chose to support AmeriCorps volunteers over the "so-called professional corps like Teach for America." On July 11, 2003, Wendy Kopp, the founder of Teach for America, received the news that $12.5 million used for scholarships and $1.5 million used for operating expenditures would not be forthcoming in the federal budget. The reason given was that the Teach for America request for funding from AmeriCorps had not been accepted. Joe Klein closed a *Time* magazine article on this issue by describing the current status of AmeriCorps:

> Wendy Kopp has 3,200 TFA members recruited so far who will not be receiving scholarship money this year. More broadly, AmeriCorps itself faces a reduction from approximately 55,000 to 35,000 members. Just before the summer recess, the Senate passed a $100 million appropriation to restore these cuts, but House majority leader Tom DeLay—who has made no secret of his desire to kill AmeriCorps—blocked the money. The President says he wants the funds restored, but he doesn't seem to have much control over the powerful DeLay. Even if Bush means what he says, Teach for America has been axed for 2003. I called the First Lady's office to see what she thought about that. She was unavailable for comment.[36]

While Teach for America struggles with financial problems, other alternative teacher education programs have flourished during the past two decades. In many areas of the country they have become a necessity because of the shortage of certified teachers. This problem has occurred primarily in urban and rural areas, but even in some suburbs there has been a lack of qualified candidates, especially in the fields of math, science, foreign languages, vocational education, and, in some communities, special education.

By 2002, forty-five states had initiated alternative teacher education programs. The 2003 federal budget included $2.85 billion dollars for a new Teacher Quality State Grants Program under Title II of the Elementary and Secondary Education Act. Included is a provision allowing funds to be used to "recruit qualified professionals from other fields . . . and provide such professionals with alternate routes to teacher certification." With the added financial support, the number of such programs is likely to grow.[37]

By January 1, 2004, New York State alone had accredited twenty such programs. Of these, fifteen are being operated by colleges in New York City. Programs throughout the nation have banded together to form an organization called the National Association for Alternative Certification. The group holds a national convention and has established its own journal (www.alt-teachercert.org/journal.htm). The Association is now offering scholarships for needy students who wish to enter alternative education programs. An example of program entrance requirements for potential candidates might include such things as a GPA of 3.0 or higher, a college major in the secondary subject to be taught, and successful completion of state certification examinations in the content areas. In addition, most programs would require an interview and possibly a writing sample.[38] Frequently candidates already have a master's degree in their field and sometimes even a doctorate.

The future of such programs is dependent on a number of factors. As long as there is a need for teachers in specific subjects and in certain academic disciplines, there will be motivation for colleges and state governments to establish alternative teacher education opportunities. Such initiatives will undoubtedly continue to have vocal detractors. Teacher education groups representing traditional programs will speak out against what many of them consider inferior "shortcut" programs. A crucial voice in this ongoing debate will be the powerful teachers' unions. These organizations sometimes see teacher shortages as a positive factor that aids them in salary negotiations. At the same time, any professional organization is likely to have reservations about what they might consider to be inadequate preparation programs. Finally, there will be additional research done on the effectiveness and retention of those teachers who entered the profession as a result of alternative certification programs. This research will undoubtedly color the debate in the years ahead.

One last recommendation made in the *A Nation at Risk* report was that "incentives, such as grants and loans, should be made available to attract outstanding students to the teaching profession, particularly in those areas of critical shortage.[39] By 2001, twenty-seven states offered financial incentives to help recruit qualified candidates into the teaching profession. Many of these programs target teachers entering specific fields or minority candidates.[40] Even with these efforts in place, our nation is still a long way from placing a qualified teacher in every classroom.

It is certainly true that since 1983 a great deal of effort and money has been expended to improve the teaching profession. As we have seen, attempts have been made to implement each of the recommendations concerning teachers mentioned in the *A Nation at Risk* report. Still, twenty years later we have a significant number of teachers lacking appropriate training and certification. In this regard we are probably not any better off than we were in 1983. The problem is likely to continue, as the United States Department of Labor predicts that

job opportunities for teachers over the next 10 years should be excellent, attributable mostly to the large number of teachers expected to retire. Although employment of preschool, kindergarten, elementary, middle, and secondary school teachers is expected to increase about as fast as the average for all occupations, a large proportion will be eligible to retire by 2010, creating many vacancies, particularly at the secondary school level. . . .

Overall enrollments through 2010, a key factor in the demand for teachers, are projected to rise slowly, resulting in average employment growth for all teachers from preschool to secondary grades. However, projected enrollments vary by region. States in the South and West— particularly California, Texas, Arizona, and Georgia—will experience large enrollment increases, while states in the Northeast and Midwest may experience declines. Projected enrollments also differ by grade, with enrollments rising moderately in grades 9–12, while remaining fairly steady for all other grades over the 2000–01 period.[41]

In the coming decade the challenge will be not only to recruit more people into the teaching profession but also to convince more racial minorities to consider teaching. Currently only 14 percent of our teachers are other than Caucasian while 36 percent of the public school children in the United States are non-Caucasian. The largest proportion of minority students is found primarily in our major cities, where the percentage in some schools is over 90 percent.[42] Members of minorities frequently seek more minority teachers to serve as role models for their children.

Retention of teachers also continues to be a major problem. Many talented teachers in the United States leave the profession for other careers. Approximately 30 percent of teachers across the nation, and 50 percent in urban schools, leave within five years. One study concluded that low compensation was "the primary cause" for this attrition.[43] Neither the problem of retention nor the practice of hiring insufficiently prepared teachers is as great an issue in Japan or in many European countries. Perhaps we can learn from these school systems. In Japan, for instance, there appears to be a "culture of coherent professional support." Teaching in Japan is a respected and well-paid profession.[44] While salaries for teachers have increased in many other countries, as noted earlier, in most localities in the United States compensation has not kept up with the rate of inflation. This is true despite the significant increase in overall educational spending at all levels. Even though there are many who claim that "throwing money at the problem" will do no good, it would appear that the matter of teacher compensation remains an issue that our society should address.

Taken as a whole, it is hard to see that a great deal of progress has been made in meeting a major objective of A Nation at Risk, which was "to make teaching a more rewarding and respected profession."[45] At best, we can say that teachers in some districts are receiving middle-class salaries and often above-average fringe benefits. In a number of affluent suburbs, teachers are approaching an annual income of $100,000. Still, we have private school teachers whose incomes are considerably less than $20,000 per year and public school faculty who earn little more than $20,000 annually. This discrepancy is in large part a function of how we currently finance education in the United States. This is an important topic that is considered in a future chapter.

Whatever the salaries may be, it is also true that in every school there are faculty members who are among the most respected and perhaps loved members in their community. This has always been true, and teachers will remain an important segment of our population and will continue to have a major influence in our society. However, teachers are not the only school employees who will affect our nation's future. At this point in our discussion it would seem an appropriate time to turn from those who teach to those who administer our schools.

NOTES

1. U.S. Department of Education, The National Commission on Excellence in Education, *A Nation at Risk: The Imperative for Educational Reform*, April 1983, Findings, 3.

2. Myra Pollack Sadker and David Miller Sadker, *Teachers, Schools, and Society* (Boston: McGraw-Hill, 2003), 596.

3. National Research Council, *Testing Teacher Candidates: The Role of Licensure Tests in Improving Teacher Quality* (Washington, D.C.: National Academy Press, 2001).

4. U.S. Department of Education, *A Nation at Risk*, Findings, 3–4.

5. David T. Gordon, ed., *A Nation Reformed?* (Cambridge, MA: Harvard Education Press, 2003), 74.

6. Pam Grossman, "Teaching: From a Nation at Risk to a Profession at Risk?" *Harvard Education Letter* 19, no.1 (January/February 2003): 2.

7. For an overview of this research, see Suzanne M. Wilson, Robert E. Floden, and Joan Ferrini-Mundy, *Teacher Preparation Research: Correct Knowledge, Gaps, and Recommendations* (Seattle: Center for the Study of Teaching and Policy, University of Washington, 2001).

8. Andrea Livingston, ed., *The Condition of Education 2003* (Washington D.C.: U.S. Department of Education, 2003), viii.

9. National Board for Professional Teaching Standards, "Why America Needs NBCTs," *Education Reform*, www.nbpts.org/edreform/why.cfm (accessed 16 December 2003).

10. National Board for Professional Teaching Standards, www.nbpts.org.

11. U.S. Department of Education, *A Nation at Risk*, Recommendations, 5.

12. National Board for Professional Teaching Standards, "Why America Needs NBCTs."

13. U.S. Department of Education, *A Nation at Risk*, Recommendation, 5.

14. Sadker and Sadker, *Teachers, Schools, and Society*, 23.

15. Sadker and Sadker, *Teachers, Schools, and Society*, 23.

16. Brian Crosby, *The $100,000 Teacher* (Sterling, VA: Capital Books, 2002), 140.

17. U.S. Department of Education, *A Nation at Risk*, Recommendations, 5.

18. Gordon, *A Nation Reformed?*, 76.

19. Gordon, *A Nation Reformed?*, 77.

20. Crosby, *The $100,000 Teacher*, 84–85.

21. Crosby, *The $100,000 Teacher*, 89.

22. Crosby, *The $100,000 Teacher*, 86.

23. U.S. Department of Education, *A Nation at Risk*, Recommendations, 5.

24. Ellen Nakashima, "Montgomery Teachers May Face Peer Review," *Washington Post*, 2 January 1999, B–1, B–6.

25. U.S. Department of Education, *A Nation at Risk*, Recommendations, 5.

26. Jay Matthews, "A New Page of Mentoring," *Washington Post*, 16 May 2000, www.washingtonpost.com/ac2/wp-dyn?pagename=article&node=&contentId=A69 (accessed 31 December 2003).

27. Matthews, "A New Page of Mentoring."

28. U.S. Department of Education, *A Nation at Risk*, Recommendations, 5.

29. U.S. Department of Education, *A Nation at Risk*, Recommendations, 5.

30. Teach for America, "Meet our Corps," *Teach For America*, www.teach foramerica.org/meet_corps.html (accessed 2 January 2004).

31. Margaret Raymond and Stephen Fletcher, "Teach for America," *Education Next*, www.educationnext.org/20021/62.html (accessed 2 January 2004), 2.

32. Raymond and Fletcher, "Teach for America," 10.

33. Raymond and Fletcher, "Teach for America," 2.

34. Sadker and Sadker, *Teachers, Schools, and Society*, 19.

35. Raymond and Fletcher, "Teach for America," 11.

36. Joe Klein, "Who Killed Teach for America?" *Time*, 17 August 2003, www.time.com/time/columnist/klein/article/0,9565,476274,00.html (accessed 2 January 2004).

37. C. Emily Feistritzer, "Alternative Teacher Certification: New Support and New Urgency," *National Council on Teacher Quality*, 18 June 2002, www.nctq .org/press/2002_consumers_guide/feistritzer.html (accessed 2 January 2004).

38. Roberts Wesleyan College, *Teachers for Tomorrow Program* (Transitional B Certification Program, 2003).

39. U.S. Department of Education, *A Nation at Risk*, Recommendations, 5.

40. Network News, "Focus on Resources for Enhancing the Teaching Profession," *Network News* 20, no. 1, (June 2001): 3.

41. U.S. Department of Labor, "Teachers—Preschool, Kindergarten, Elementary, Middle, and Secondary," *U.S. Department of Labor: Bureau of Labor Statistics Occupational Outlook Handbook*, http://bls.gov/oco/ocos069.htm (accessed 2 January 2004), 7–8.

42. Chrystal Griffin, "Diverse Education: Minorities Scarce in Teaching Jobs," *The State News* (2004), www.statenews.com/article.phtml?pk=14342 (accessed 2 January 2004).

43. Arthur E. Wise, "It's Retention," *Quality Teaching* (Fall 2002): 3.

44. Wise, "It's Retention," 3.

45. U.S. Department of Education, *A Nation at Risk*, Recommendations, 5.

CHAPTER 9

The Administrators

Effective leadership is essential to any organization. One of the Implementing Recommendations in the *A Nation at Risk* report was that "principals and superintendents must play a crucial role in developing school and community support for the reforms we propose."[1] Certainly it is true that administrators need to participate in and support any changes made in our schools. This is especially important with recommendations emanating from the national or state governments. Like teacher unions, individual school administrators, as well as their state and national organizations, can be impediments to carrying out new initiatives. This being the case, it is instructive to look carefully at the developments in the school administration field during the past two decades. We begin with the chief school officer.

Superintendents have numerous official and legal responsibilities along with a number of ceremonial roles. As the chief full-time leader of the school district, the superintendent is responsible for recruiting, selecting, and recommending to the board of education the employment of all district personnel. In addition, the chief school officer must oversee programs for personnel supervision, evaluation, and professional growth. Most states give the superintendent the duty of recommending or not recommending teacher and administrator tenure appointments to the board of education. The superintendent or a designee must negotiate and manage contracts with all employee groups in the district. An essential management function is to prepare, present, and implement the school budget.

On the academic side, the chief school officer also is expected to introduce new programs to the board of education and evaluate those already in place. It would be the superintendent who would oversee the process of developing new curriculum offerings in any of the schools in the district. Aside from curriculum and management duties, the superintendent is responsible for community outreach and district public relations. Along with the ceremonial tasks at graduation and other school functions, it is usually the chief school officer who is the primary spokesperson for the school with community groups and government agencies, as well as the media. Because of these many diverse roles, superintendents must demonstrate a variety of political skills both within the schools and in the community.

To be effective, a district leader must be articulate and have the ability to be persuasive in both large and small groups. He or she should be a good listener who is sensitive to the opinions of others and be able to guide groups in making consensus decisions. To carry out agreed-upon programs, a superintendent must have planning skills and the ability to motivate community members, faculty, and staff. Being politically savvy is associated by some with the field of politics, which unfortunately has a negative connotation for many people in our society. Still, it is important that we remember that in a democracy decisions are made in a political setting. A leader who is able to work with groups of people in the process of reaching a collective decision can make a valuable contribution in any organization. At the same time, being skillful politically is not enough to assure a superintendent's success.

As the primary advisor to the board of education, chief school officers should also be able to offer a vision as to what the school district can become. A leader must know where he or she is leading. Chief school officers should have some firm convictions as to what is essential in developing an excellent educational program. Even a superintendent with vision and political skills needs an additional characteristic to ensure success. Without integrity, administrators eventually lose the confidence of their staff and the community. Chief school officers should provide a model of personal honesty if they are to earn the respect of the many diverse constituencies who have an interest in the schools. Finally, it certainly helps to have a sense of humor and not to be overly sensitive to criticism. Serving as a school superintendent is not an easy job. The good news is that chief school officers are able to make major contributions in their communities and to earn the gratitude and respect of many people.

It is also true that during the past twenty years superintendents' salaries and fringe benefits have improved dramatically.

On the other hand, the job has become increasingly more difficult. This is one of the reasons for the high turnover rate among chief school officers. In our major cities, the average tenure has been calculated as approximately three years. New York City had twelve superintendents in twenty years, while Kansas City has gone through eighteen chief school officers in thirty years.[2] Needless to say, it is not easy for any executive to have a major impact in such a short time. Although in rural and suburban districts the turnover rate is approximately five to six years, it is still not a long tenure in an important leadership role. It is also true that, because superintendents are beginning to serve in the position at a later point in their career, their time on the job will be limited, especially if they choose an early retirement. In a study published in 2000, 92 percent of the superintendents surveyed believed that "high turnover in the superintendency is a serious crisis in American education."[3] By explaining some of the factors surrounding the high turnover rate, it is possible to identify some ways for dealing with the problem.

It is not surprising that at a time when schools are being held more accountable superintendents will become a focus of community discussion. When comparative test scores are less than impressive, the chief school officer must not only offer an explanation but also propose viable solutions. Like a business that fails to make a profit, a school district that does not improve test scores can expect criticism from their constituents. Especially in urban areas where there are constant financial problems, it is extremely difficult for superintendents to bring about dramatic improvements. Today the pressure for school choice and the growth of charter schools in many states creates another challenge, especially for urban superintendents.

There are several groups that can impede a superintendent's efforts to bring about positive change in a district. Because the chief school officer is responsible directly to the board of education, an appropriate relationship between the superintendent and the members of the board is absolutely necessary. Both the board and the superintendent play crucial roles in the administration of the school district. Theoretically, the board establishes policy, and the superintendent is responsible for administering this policy. Realistically, as a full-time professional specialist, the chief school officer is expected to make recommendations for board approval. The challenge is to develop a relationship in which the board is much more than a "rubber stamp" for the superintendent, but does not try to "micromanage" the district. The line between policymaking and administration is not always clear. The skilled superintendent can work with the board to create a team that will be mutually supportive. Unfortunately this does not always happen.

Veteran and retired administrators frequently talk about how boards of education have changed. They mention the increase in the number of "single issue" candidates. For instance, some people run for the board primarily to lower taxes, while others wish to make a single change in the district, such as the removal of the superintendent. Even when a positive relationship exists between the superintendent and the board, the superintendent must also work to ensure a working partnership with employee groups. This is especially important with the teacher union in the district. In some communities the leader of the teachers' union rivals the superintendent in public exposure and in the power to mobilize teachers for or against a proposed change. The relationship between the superintendent and the head of the union is sometimes strained because the chief school officer is frequently the spokesperson for the board when financial restraint is necessary. The problem is especially difficult when new salary agreements are being negotiated. While the superintendent may sometimes be sympathetic with the union's demands, he or she must communicate the position of the board of education. In doing so, a chief school officer can sometimes lose the trust and support of employees of the district.

Another factor complicating the work of school administrators is the increasingly complex nature of school governance in the United States. For much of the twentieth century, schools have been under the control of local and state governments. Today the courts and the federal government have become much more important in setting policies and creating legal mandates for schools. Superintendents are more frequently involved in lawsuits, and in the twenty-first century they are undoubtedly going to be spending a great deal of effort in implementing the No Child Left Behind law which was passed and signed in 2002.

Superintendents will also need to deal with an ever-increasing diversity in their student bodies as well as more students with limited language proficiency. Special education laws and court decisions have also touched every public school in the country. This problem has become greater as more and more districts attempt to carry out a policy of integrating special education students in regular classrooms (inclusion). Of course there is also the added challenge of introducing technology into the offices and classrooms of our schools. All of these factors have made the position of the superintendent of schools one of the most challenging in today's society. While the job has changed, we have been slow in altering the way we prepare people to become superintendents.

One of the major issues is whether or not chief school officers should continue to be chosen from those who have gone through a traditional preparation program. In the past, the most frequent career pattern has been for candidates to first gain experience as a teacher and then as a lower level administrator. For most, this meant a number of years working as a principal or perhaps an assistant superintendent. In addition, states have almost all required additional course work in school administration. More recently, these programs have required one or more internships in school districts. Some states have more restricted career patterns and educational requirements than others. For instance, in Pennsylvania, the requirements for a school superintendent include six years of teaching or serving in some other administrative role in a school (guidance counselor, administrator). During three of these years, candidates must hold a public school certificate. Superintendents must also have the equivalent of a two-year graduate-level degree in educational administration in a state-approved program. In Indiana, along with two years of teaching experience, a superintendent must earn a doctorate and pass a written examination. Massachusetts requires three years of school administrative experience along with passing an examination. In Minnesota, three years of teaching experience and a graduate program that includes an internship of 320 hours in continuous months is required.[4]

There have been a number of critics who have pointed out weaknesses in how educational administrators are trained and chosen. One such critic, Marc Tucker, has written that "university-based school administration programs are incoherent, undercapitalized, and disconnected from the districts where graduates are most likely to seek employment. There is much to be learned from the way business and the military train their leaders."[5] Tucker and others have called for drawing leadership talent from outside of education to run our school districts.

Already a number of large city districts have selected superintendents who have not had the experience of working in the schools or having taken educational administration classes. This practice has had mixed results. Perhaps the best-known example is the career of John Sanford in Seattle. A retired major general and county executive, Sanford was given credit for bringing about great improvements in the Seattle district. During his brief three-year tenure he earned the respect of the citizens of the city as well as his colleagues throughout the nation. When he became critically ill and eventually died, there was an outpouring of sympathy which became a story in the national media. His accomplishments in a difficult district are an example of how someone from outside education can succeed as a superintendent. During the same period, David Hornbeck had a much more difficult time. A minister and lawyer prior to becoming the superintendent of schools in Philadelphia, Hornbeck's tenure was characterized by strife with the teachers' union and institutional gridlock.[6] More recently, Philadelphia has hired Paul Vallas as the chief executive of the Philadelphia city schools. Although he has only been there a short time, he is receiving excellent press reviews for the changes he is making in this troubled district.[7] The conflict inherent in large city superintendencies is illustrated by Mr. Vallas' career prior to going to Philadelphia. A government official before being named the superintendent in Chicago, Mr. Vallas was given credit along with Mayor Richard Daley for dramatic improvements in the Chicago schools. Unfortunately, after a turbulent six years in Chicago, it was rumored that Vallas was forced to leave the district.[8]

The practice of hiring as a superintendent of schools someone who has not worked in a school system thus far has occurred primarily in very large cities. This probably is defensible because in large cities a superintendent has numerous assistants who can act as specialists in academic areas. In a small rural district, a superintendent is expected to be personally involved in curriculum issues and in teacher tenure decisions. In any case, some states are considering creating ways that individuals from outside education can quickly become eligible to be school administrators. Even with this trend, it is likely that most of our school superintendents in the near future will continue to follow a more traditional career pattern. This being the case, colleges and universities should be seeking to improve their school administration programs. There are several steps that might be taken to meet this objective.

First of all, future administrators should experience a planned program rather than merely accumulating a specific number of educational administration courses. Such a program should include classes and experiences in leadership, school finance, school law, curriculum, and assessment. Any planned curriculum for school administrators should also mandate one or more realistic internship experiences. The courses themselves should offer problem-solving experiences utilizing real-life case studies. Once a new administrator is hired, a formal mentor should be available to help the new manager during the first year on the job. School districts should also strongly urge that their administrative staff participate in ongoing professional-growth programs that consist of more than annual attendance at an administrative convention.

Special attention must be paid not only to the preparation of future superintendents but to perhaps the even more crucial need to recruit and train outstanding principals. The broad scope of a principal's job can be seen in the description used by the U.S. Department of Labor, which lists the duties as follows.

1. Principals set the academic tone of the school building. They are involved in hiring, evaluating, and helping to improve the skills of teachers and other staff.
2. Principals are part of a district administrative team and also work with students, parents, and representatives of community organizations. Principals must work with all of these groups in making administrative decisions.
3. Principals are responsible for budgets, schedules, and numerous reports.
4. Principals are accountable for students' academic progress and for ensuring that their teachers are following appropriate curriculums.
5. Principals are important in the establishment of a healthy and safe school climate. As part of this responsibility, they must maintain discipline among the student body.[9]

Problems related to the preparation of principals are similar to those facing colleges and universities as they train superintendents. This issue is perhaps different in the fact that the role of the school principal has been changing during the past two decades. Historically, a principal has been primarily a manager and a disciplinarian. In the past, a successful building administrator had only to maintain a school of well-disciplined students, keep the faculty and staff relatively happy, and not upset the parents. High-stakes testing and school accountability has added a new dimension to the position. Currently a principal must also now provide leadership in an academic program that will continually improve student learning as well as provide growth opportunities for faculty and staff. If standardized test scores fail to improve in any school building, there will be pressure on the school's administrator from the central office, the board of education, and eventually from the community. To be an instructional leader, a principal must have some knowledge in all areas of curriculum, research-proven teaching techniques, child development, and group decision-making skills. It is no longer easy to move directly from the classroom into administering a school. There is no question that we must do a better job in preparing those who will be leading our schools in the twenty-first century.

The literature is filled with studies showing the problems school districts are having in finding qualified people to administer their school buildings.[10] There are several reasons for the lack of candidates. Increasingly teachers observe the problems that their principals face and decide that it is more enjoyable to remain a classroom teacher. The fact that veteran teachers can make as much or more money than someone beginning educational administration as an assistant principal discourages other potential candidates. The additional responsibility of working during school vacations, having evening obligations, and often being employed during the summer also discourages many individuals. To pursue a position in administration, the teacher most often needs to spend money on graduate courses and give up the necessary evenings to attend classes and complete assignments. Most certification programs require that future administrators also serve in an internship, which can complicate one's personal schedule.

In order to motivate qualified teachers to prepare for administration, school districts will need to take several steps. It certainly would be helpful to raise the salaries of both assistant principals and principals. To make the job manageable, a principal should have sufficient support personnel. This means that schools must consider appointing assistant principals as well as an adequate number of counselors, psychologists, and social workers. Some districts will agree to pay for the graduate work of those teachers in their schools who pursue certification in administration. Other larger districts are cooperating with area colleges to set up programs for their faculty members who show leadership potential.

Another reality that is shaping the current need for principals is the high rate of turnover. Some of this problem is caused by administrators who leave their position to move up the administrative ladder. This tendency is not likely to change, especially if the principal's job is not better compensated and made more manageable. There are many principals who love being close to students and teachers and who see the challenge of administrating a school as a lifelong calling. We need to make sure that these people are properly recognized and rewarded for the work they are doing. As a nation we must face the fact that the need for principals has never been greater: "40 percent of the nation's 93,200 principals are nearing retirement, according to the Department of Labor, and 42 percent of the surveyed districts say they already have a shortage of qualified candidates for open principal positions."[11] The above factors, coupled with the growing tendency of school administrators to retire early, ensures that we face an ongoing shortage in the years ahead.

One can only conclude after considering the current status of educational administration in the United States that there is much work to be done. As a nation, we must do a better job of recruiting, training, selecting, and supporting those who step forward to become educational leaders. There is no question that part of the responsibility for carrying out these tasks belongs with individual boards of education. The *A Nation at Risk* report states that

> school boards must provide them with the professional development and support required to carry out their leadership role effectively. The Commission stresses the distinction between leadership skills involving persuasion, setting goals and developing community consensus behind them, and managerial and supervisory skills. Although the latter are necessary, we believe that school boards must consciously develop leadership skills at the school and district levels if the reforms we propose are to be achieved.[12]

This is only one of the crucial roles that boards of education must play if we are to improve our public schools.

NOTES

1. U.S. Department of Education, The National Commission on Excellence in Education, *A Nation at Risk: The Imperative for Educational Reform*, April 1983, Leadership and Fiscal Report, 5.

2. Tamara Henry, "Superintendents in Demand," *USA Today*, sec. A, p. 1, 26 January 2000.

3. Tamara Henry, "Superintendents in Demand," sec. A, p. 2.

4. Frederick M. Hess, "Lifting the Barrier," *Education Next*, Fall 2003, 17.

5. Marc Tucker, "Out with the Old," *Education Next*, Fall 2003, 20.

6. *The Merrill Report* (Alexandria Virginia: Public Broadcasting Service, 1999), television program.

7. Michael Dobbs, "At the Heart of Reform," *The Washington Post National Weekly Addition*, 12–18 January 2004, 31.

8. Alexander Russo, "Political Educator," *Education Next*, Winter 2003, www.educationext.org/20031/38.html (accessed 23 January 2003).

9. U.S. Department of Labor, "Educational Administrators," *U.S. Department of Labor Bureau of Labor Statistics Occupational Outlook Handbook*, http://stats.bls.gov/oco/ocos007.htm (accessed 1 February 2003).

10. Robin Rayfield and Tom Diamantes, "Principal Satisfaction and the Shortage of Education Leaders," *Connections* 5, 24 December 2003, www.principals.org/publications/connections/rayfield.cfm (accessed on 6 January 2004).

11. Craig Savoye, "Fewer Step Forward to Be School Principals," *Christian Science Monitor* 93, no. 216 (2 October 2001): 16.

12. U.S. Department of Education, *A Nation at Risk*, Recommendations, 5–6.

CHAPTER 10

The Boards

Early in the history of American education, citizens of local communities or boards of education were totally responsible for the school in their area. These groups raised the necessary funds, decided on the curriculum, and hired the teachers. It was not until near the middle of the nineteenth century that state governments become more active in helping to finance and regulate schools. Even at the outset of the twentieth century, elected board members maintained a great deal of independence in governing their schools. By 1950, state governments had become heavily engaged in public education, as a significant portion of the cost was being assumed at the state level. This state involvement was in keeping with the United States Constitution. Education is not among the powers delegated to the federal government, and it was long accepted that the responsibility for schools was reserved for the states. The Tenth Amendment of the Constitution states that "the powers not delegated to the United States by the Constitution, nor prohibited by it to the states, are reserved to the states respectively, or to the people."[1]

Despite this amendment and the long tradition of local and state supremacy over education, during the 1960s Congress began to pass legislation that would have significant impact on schools. The first major initiative came as part of President Lyndon B. Johnson's War on Poverty. The Elementary and Secondary Education Act passed in 1965 provided a major federal aid program for schools to assist them in providing remedial opportunities for students from disadvantaged homes. As a result, Title I of this act saw school districts preparing plans for government approval that would provide remediation for eligible students in the areas of reading or math. The funds were used primarily to hire special teachers to work with these children. Also included as part of the poverty initiative was the Head Start program which was designed to help underprivileged preschool children. A comprehensive program, Head Start not only provides classes for eligible children from age three to five, but it also has a component to help keep the children healthy as well as special training opportunities for the parents of these children.

In 1975 the federal government entered further into the field of education with the passage of Public Law 94-142, the Education for All Handicapped Children Act. This law was replaced in 1991 by the Individuals with Disabilities Education Act (IDEA). These laws require schools to identify and offer services to children, from birth to age twenty-one, who are found by a local committee to be in need of special education services. No matter the severity of the disability, school districts were mandated by the federal government to provide an appropriate individualized program in the "least restrictive environment." This phrase has come to mean that an identified child should be placed in a learning setting that is as close as possible to a regular classroom containing nonhandicapped students. Today, approximately 11 percent of students enrolled in public schools have been found to be in need of some sort of special education service. For each of these children, there is also the requirement that an Individualized Education Plan (IEP) be developed and followed closely. Although such a law was needed to ensure that students with unique problems be given special consideration in our schools, for the last twenty-five years, meeting the requirements of the law has cost billions of dollars and created a cadre of special education teachers, specialists such as physical therapists, occupational therapists, and speech and hearing specialists. In addition, the mandate for maintaining complete records of these students and the required due process procedure necessary in placement decisions has created a whole new bureaucracy in every school district. Administration of Title I and special education programs has been a shared responsibility between the states and federal government. For the most part, local boards of education had little influence over these new mandates. Even with these and other federal initiatives, the federal government still furnishes only about 7 percent of the total revenue used to support public education in the United States.

Depending on national politics, this could change. Supported by the two powerful national teachers' unions, the National Education Association and the American Federation of Teachers, the Democratic Party has for several decades supported increased national funding of education. During the last quarter of the twentieth century, the Republican Party has usually taken the position that schools should remain primarily the responsibility of state and local government.

While Republicans have been resisting major new federal initiatives in the field of education, they have been supporting the idea that parents should have a choice when enrolling students in school. Whether it be charter schools or the more controversial voucher system, many Republicans have argued that competition would increase the effectiveness of all schools. Upon taking office in 2001, President George W. Bush still supported school choice, but in a major political compromise in 2002, which also received the support of many Democrats, Congress passed the No Child Left Behind Act. Some Democrats who were skeptical voted for the bill because it would allegedly increase federal financial aid to schools dramatically. This comprehensive law, which is discussed in detail in chapter 16, also will undoubtedly affect the prerogatives of local school boards. Even with this new legislation, it would be a mistake to believe that state and federal initiatives in education have stripped local school boards of all their powers.

To begin with, it is the local board that personally selects the chief school officer who will administer the school system. In some smaller districts, boards sometimes have active input into hiring school principals. Legally, they must also agree to the employment of all school personnel, and in most states board approval is required in tenure appointments for teachers and some administrators.

As part of their responsibility for personnel, board members must approve of contracts for all employee groups. These contracts deal not only with the issues of salary and fringe benefits, but possibly also with provisions concerning topics such as class size, teacher evaluation, and even the school calendar. In some districts, board members are actively involved in negotiations and sometimes even participate at the bargaining table.

Perhaps the most significant power that still resides in the local community is the development and passage of the school-district budget. Even though much of the preparation work is done by administrators, an engaged board of education will significantly affect priorities in the district. Decisions on whether to attempt to lower class size, hire more teacher aides, or increase the number of electives all are likely to be topics discussed at board meetings. They might have to decide whether the district should buy new football uniforms or allot available funds for computers or perhaps library books. In addition, the elected local officials are responsible for maintaining the school facilities. They will make crucial decisions about closing a school or building a new one. Board policies will also affect whether the school is providing a safe and orderly environment for its students. Boards of education will decide whether the district should adopt strict disciplinary policies, hire security guards, or perhaps spend money to hire additional counselors to work with troubled students.

Even though curriculum decisions are being made more and more at the state level because of the standards movement and high-stakes testing, it is still the local school districts that determine elective offerings and extracurricular activities. Boards of education must determine whether to introduce a program for gifted and talented students, which might include hiring special teachers to provide "pull-out" programs or perhaps offering an array of Advanced Placement or other college courses. In addition, the local board must decide on the extent of extracurricular programs and whether limited funds should be spent for athletics or a student newspaper.

Finally, elected board of education members are important in maintaining effective communication within a school district. They are available to citizens who have suggestions or concerns related to any school program. Board members also can be informed advocates for the school system and attempt to increase public support for schools. Because of these many functions, boards of education remain an important force in our nation's effort to improve our schools.

Despite the importance of the job, many observers have suggested that, as with other local leadership offices, it is becoming more difficult to find committed and qualified candidates for positions on a board of education. At one time, respected and responsible individuals from the community saw board membership as a way that they could provide a voluntary service in their community. It was common for people who had been well educated themselves and successful in their professions to offer themselves for election to the school board. Thus in many communities board members included prominent professionals and business leaders.

In recent years, board membership has become a more demanding position that lacks a high degree of respect in many communities. School districts that have seen conflict over budgets or with employee groups have become a battleground. It is not unusual for meetings to become confrontational. Especially when there is an issue dividing the community, large numbers of citizens, parents, school employees, and even students will be in attendance. This type of meeting is usually well covered by the media, and many districts now have their meetings broadcast on local radio or television stations. This increase in conflict and visibility has undoubtedly caused some individuals, who in the past might have considered board membership, to seek other, less stressful ways to involve themselves in public service.

Although it is difficult to prove, many experienced administrators have observed that those choosing to seek board membership have changed in recent years. Instead of respected community leaders, there are now many more "single-issue" candidates seeking election. These individuals can be representatives of taxpayer leagues who have as their sole objective control over the local property tax rate, or they may be people who wish to use board membership to champion their own pet programs. Parents representing gifted and talented students or special education students may well become candidates to lobby for the needs of their own children. In some places, individuals might run simply to make a change in school district personnel.

There is not only a potential problem with the motivation for some candidates, but even more disturbing is the fact that in some districts it is difficult to entice anyone to run for the board. Frequently there is no contest in board elections because of the lack of candidates. This lack of interest results often in discouraging voter turnouts for many school board elections. In too many places less than 10 percent of the registered voters are participating in elections. A related problem is the increasingly high turnover rate among board members, with many choosing to serve only one term. Because of the complexities of many of the issues, there is a lengthy learning curve for new board members. One administrator has commented that "for the first year, board members are expected to be stupid, but after that it is optional."

The fact is that many new board members come to their position with little or no preparation. They are then quickly asked to help make decisions on difficult issues with little background information. The responsibility for orienting new board members lies primarily with the superintendent of schools and perhaps the board president. Local, state, and national organizations do provide training for new and veteran board members. In order to effectively do their job, it is also important that the school administration provide board members with significant background research on issues facing the community. On the other hand, it is essential that board members do their homework and ask the right questions before voting on an issue. Board members must also take the initiative to attend training sessions and make themselves available to the community. As elected representatives, they need to know what is happening in the schools as well as what their constituents are thinking.

Most of all, board members must develop a mindset that they are part of a team that has a significant obligation to provide a quality education to the children of the community. District employees should be seen as partners, as opposed to being considered as the opposition. There are positive indications that boards and district employee unions are working together more peacefully than in the past. Teachers' unions have been making an effort to increase the professionalism of teachers, and there have been examples in many districts of positive cooperation between boards of education and their employees. Some of these improved feelings may be lost, as state governments currently lack the funds to increase state aid to local schools. Many boards are likely to become hesitant about making up the difference by raising local property taxes. Unfortunately, the result could be increased difficulty in reaching contract settlements. When this happens we might expect to see more picket signs and even strikes.

Hopefully these things will not happen and districts will find new ways to work together to bring about positive change. The challenge for boards of education will be to continue to find and carry out their appropriate role within the school district. Boards can move too far to one extreme or the other in carrying out their duties. Generally it is accepted that it is the job of the elected representatives of the district to develop school district policy, and it is the role of administrators to carry out these decisions. In practice it is not that simple. Some boards become overly involved in the day-to-day routine of the school district. When this happens, administrators and other staff are made uncomfortable by what has been labeled "micromanagement." The opposite problem occurs when boards of education are seen by the community as merely a "rubber stamp" for the administration. If a board is perceived either as "micromanagers" or a "rubber stamp," they will lose the respect of either the employees or the community.

Although it is important that boards of education maintain the support of both the employees of the district and the community, it is essential that they be aware that their primary constituents are the students. The importance of this fact is contained in a publication of the California School Boards Association, which included this statement:

> As the only locally elected officials chosen to represent the interest of school children, board members have a responsibility to speak out on behalf of the children in their community. Boards are advocates for their students, their districts' educational programs and public education. They build support within their communities and at the state and national levels.[2]

In order to carry out their vital functions, board members would be wise to consider the guidelines provided by the New York State School Boards Association:

1. Boards must exercise their duties in compliance with state and federal law.
2. Members of Boards of Education must act as a unit rather than as individual members.
3. Members of Boards of Education must maintain strong ethical standards and avoid conflicts of interest in performing their duties.
4. A Board of Education must develop clear rules for their meetings. Included should be provision for prepublished agendas, complete minutes that are made available to all citizens, and provisions for public participation in the work of the board.[3]

A final source of assistance for boards has been provided by the Iowa Association of School Boards when it published a list of characteristics of successful board members:

They work well as members of a team.
- They understand that the board, rather than individuals on the board, establishes the policies and makes the decisions that provide direction for the school district.
- They collaborate with staff, families, other agencies and businesses to build schools that encourage the best from all students.
- They work to improve schools by building public understanding, support and participation.

They focus their efforts on serving all children.
- They make sure every deliberation, decision or action of the board takes into consideration the best interests of all the students they serve.
- They understand board members are entrusted by all the parents in the community and that no child is more important than another.

They realize demeanor has consequences and act accordingly.
- They understand that the way board members act as individuals and as a body affects the climate of the school district.
- They are respectful, listening carefully to colleagues, staff, parents and the public.
- They have integrity and display professionalism, setting a tone for the schools that communicates the importance and seriousness of their work.
- They operate with fairness and sustained effort so that long-term changes can be implemented. They focus on student achievement no matter what issues arise.

They respect the diversity of perspectives and styles on the board and in the community.
- They know their board is as diverse as the community it serves.
- They respect their fellow board members' right to hold differing views.[4]

Carrying out successfully the role of a member of a board of education is not a simple task. Frustration and even anger can easily overcome the best intentions. Still, it is undoubtedly true that despite the increasing role of state and federal government in our schools, local control of education remains a popular sentiment in the United States. Our history and tradition of local boards of education will continue into the twenty-first century. Any major initiatives to reform our system will be affected by decisions made at the local level. However, if children are to become better educated, schools themselves are only part of the answer. Even before they enter kindergarten, children have been greatly affected by what they have been taught at home. Parents will continue to significantly affect their children's success in schools. For this reason, it is essential that parents become active partners in educational reform.

NOTES

1. Robert L. Hardgrave Jr., *American Government* (Orlando: Harcourt Brace Jovanovich, 1986), 89.

2. California School Boards Association, "School Board Leadership: The Role and Function of California's School Boards," 21 September 2000, www.csba.org/communications/leadership/lead.htm.

3. New York State School Boards Association, "Essential Roles and Responsibilities," 8 September 2000, www.nyssba.org/bdsupport/essential.htm.

4. Iowa Association of School Boards, "Traits of Effective School Board Members," www.ia-sb.org/boardbasics/traits.asp (accessed 6 June 2004).

CHAPTER 11

The Parents

The authors of the *A Nation at Risk* report acknowledge the role that parents play in the education of their children with these words: "The task of assuring the success of our recommendations does not fall to the schools and colleges alone. Obviously, faculty members and administrators, along with policymakers and the mass media, will play a crucial role in the reform of the educational system. But even more important is the role of parents and students, and to them we speak directly."[1] In the two paragraphs that follow these words, parents are given these instructions:

- Parents "must possess a deep respect for intelligence, achievement, and learning, and the skills needed to use them."
- Parents have "the right to demand for [their] children the best our schools and colleges can provide."
- Parents are a child's "first and most influential teacher," and they must be a *"living* example" of what they expect their children to honor and emulate.
- Parents must "nurture [their] child's curiosity, creativity, and confidence" and be "active participants in the work of schools."
- Parents themselves must be lifelong learners.
- Parents must model "intellectual and moral integrity coupled with hard work and commitment."[2]

There is little question that the report was correct in emphasizing the role of parents. An educational research publication states unequivocally that the evidence is beyond dispute. When schools work together with families to support learning, children tend to succeed not just in school, but throughout life. In fact, the most accurate predictor of a student's achievement in school is not income or social status, but the extent to which that student's family is able to:

1. Create a home environment that encourages learning
2. Express high (but not unrealistic) expectations for their children's achievement and future careers
3. Become involved in their children's education at school and in the community.[3]

The same publication reports that families whose children are doing well in school exhibit the following six characteristics:

Establish a daily family routine
 Examples: Providing time and a quiet place to study, assigning responsibility for household chores, being firm about times to get up and go to bed, having dinner together
Monitor out-of-school activities
 Examples: Setting limits on TV watching, checking up on children when parents are not at home, arranging for after-school activities and supervised care
Model the value of learning, self-discipline, and hard work
 Examples: Communicating through questioning and conversation, demonstrating that achievement comes from working hard, using reference materials and the library
Express high but realistic expectations for achievement
 Examples: Setting goals and standards that are appropriate for the children's age and maturity, recognizing and encouraging special talents, informing friends and family about successes
Encourage children's development and progress in school
 Examples: Maintaining a warm and supportive home, showing interest in children's progress at school, helping with homework, discussing the value of a good education and possible career options, staying in touch with teachers and school staff
Encourage reading, writing, and discussion among family members
 Examples: Reading, listening to children read, and talking about what is being read; discussing the day over dinner; telling stories and sharing problems; writing letters, lists, and messages[4]

The well-known conservative historian of American education, Diane Ravitch, has written that there has been a decline in the amount of parental academic support for children. Writing in a chapter entitled "Children on Their Own," she points first to the trend that saw women taking more jobs outside of the home. In the same passage, she alludes to

> the erosion of adult authority, fear of litigation, the decline of the neigh- borhood school, the lessening of community cohesion, and the loss of conviction within the education profession that schools should teach children the difference between right and wrong. As parents withdrew their responsibilities, the schools lacked the capacity to take their place.[5]

According to this analysis, students were left on their own "to hang out at malls, watch television, roam the Internet, work part-time after school. . . . For many children, no one was acting in loco parentis."[6] Whether one accepts this view of the recent history of American society or not, there have been a number of significant changes in the struc- ture of American families:

- Our families are getting smaller, older, and more diverse.
- While Americans still prefer marriage, during the past quarter cen- tury, the number of unmarried opposite- and same-sex partners liv- ing together has increased from 2 to 5.5 million. Since live-in re- lationships generally last about eighteen months, the arrival and rearing of children mean less stability for everyone.[7]
- Approximately thirteen million children—one in five—live in single-parent families. . . . Research shows that children from single-parent families are less likely to achieve and more than twice as likely to drop out of school.[8]
- In 1960, 39 percent of married women with children between the ages of 6 and 17 worked outside the home; this number had in- creased to 78 percent by the late 1990s.[9]

Although the above changes have undoubtedly affected schools, to un- derstand differences in academic achievement, one must consider several other factors. Perhaps the most important variable is ethnicity. When one looks at students' grades, Asian American students do the best, usually earning a combination of As and Bs. Caucasian students are next, while African American and Hispanic students have on average lower grades.[10]

It would seem that these differences are present among all economic classes. Asian American students do well whether they are from a family with a low income or a family with a high income. This would seem to suggest that parental behavior and attitudes in these families have a significant impact on a students' success in school. Laurence Steinberg has gone so far as to suggest that school reform efforts have failed and by themselves will never bring about a significant change in academic achievement. For him at least, it is parents who have it within their power to successfully promote student learning. To do so, he believes they must do the following:

- Transform the national debate over the causes and cures of our achievement problem from one about reforming schools to one about changing students' and parents' attitudes and behaviors.
- We must make it clear in the minds of young people and parents that the primary activity of childhood and adolescence is schooling. If we want children and teenagers to value education and strive for achievement, adults must behave as if doing well in school—not just finishing school, but actually doing well in school—is more important that socializing, more important than organized sports, more important than working at after school jobs, more important than any other activity in which young people are involved.
- We must have a serious and open discussion about the high rate of parental irresponsibility in this country and the toll it is taking on youngsters' lives. Parenting skills must be taught in well-designed programs which can be sponsored by schools.
- Schools must expand their efforts to actively draw parents into school programs. This will require restructuring and rescheduling school programs to meet the needs of working parents.[11]

Parental involvement in schools is the highest at the elementary level. The National Parent Teacher Association (PTA) reports that it is actually dropping in middle schools and high schools. The Department of Education has reported that 48 percent of the children in grades K–5 had a parent who volunteered or served on a school committee. The figure was 29 percent at the middle school level and only 26 percent in high schools. Approximately 76 percent of all PTA members are affiliated with elementary schools.[12]

Anyone who has participated in many parent open houses at school cannot help but be struck by the large crowds of parents who visit the classrooms in kindergarten through grade three. At the same time, parental attendance at high school open houses is often quite sparse. This is true despite the fact that it is at the secondary level where the academic achievement of American students is most depressed when compared with other nations. Parent involvement with their children's education at any age is one of the factors that research clearly demonstrates can make a difference in student achievement. The studies done on this topic point to the following factors:

- It is important to work directly with children in the home by reading with them, "supporting work on homework assignments," and actually tutoring them using instructions and materials supplied by the teacher.
- It is helpful to support school activities by attending parent–teacher conferences, open houses, volunteering in the classroom and on field trips, and communicating directly with the teacher by phone or through notes.
- The most effective programs offering parental involvement should have an orientation or training component, but this should not be overdone.
- Schools must offer a wide range of opportunities for parental involvement because of the various schedules, interests, and abilities of parents.[13]

Perhaps the weakest aspect of many programs is that those parents who participate most actively are almost always from families where the children are succeeding in school. The challenge for schools is to engage the parents of disadvantaged students who are not doing well. Researchers have found that minority and low-income parents are less likely to be involved with their child's school. The reasons include the following:

- Lack of time or energy (due to long hours of heavy physical labor, for example)
- Embarrassment or shyness about one's own educational level or linguistic ability

- Lack of understanding or information about the structure of the school and accepted communication channels
- Perceived lack of welcome by teachers and administrators
- Teachers' and administrators' assumptions of parents' disinterest or inability to help with children's schooling.[14]

The good news is that "parents of disadvantaged and minority children can and do make a positive contribution to their children's achievement in school if they receive adequate training and encouragement in the types of parent involvement that make a difference." This is true whatever the parent's level of education. In reality, it is the disadvantaged children who have the most to gain from parent involvement programs.[15]

To carry out the objective of increasing parental involvement, there are a number of guidelines that should be kept in mind. Somehow parents must be convinced that their involvement and support will make a difference in their child's success in school. This should begin at the preschool level and continue as long as a student is attending a school. Parents should be instructed by the school on how to help their child with homework and how to monitor and encourage the learning activities of older students. Special efforts must be made to include parents of disadvantaged students who are reluctant to become involved in school. Finally, parents must be told often that their efforts are valued and needed by the school. Teachers and parents should think of themselves as partners in a student's education.[16]

Of all the groups that must be drawn into the school environment, perhaps the most important are the parents and students with limited English proficiency. Twenty percent of the young people in the United States are immigrants or the children of immigrants. These students speak over 300 different languages in their home.[17]

In an issue of *Educational Leadership*, June Cavarretta writes about a large district thirty-five miles northwest of Chicago where the per-student expenditure is one of the lowest in the area. Still, the district has trained over 400 parent volunteers to participate with teachers and administrators in shared decision making. These planning teams focus on "trust building, collaboration, shared vision, and continuous improvement." They have been responsible for establishing block scheduling, a true middle-school philosophy, and multi-age classrooms in their district.[18]

In New York State, parental involvement on site-based management teams has been mandated in every school for more than a decade. The teams, made up of administrators, teachers, and parents, have been established in every building and have brought parents into the decision-making process at both the school and district level. They have been involved in such issues as budgeting, selection of teachers, and planning extracurricular programs.

Realizing the benefits of parental involvement in school, the National PTA has supported six standards identified by Joyce Epstein of the Center on School, Family, and Community Partnerships at Johns Hopkins University. They include the following steps that "outline a process for improving parent and family involvement—and students' success":

1. *Create an action team.* Involve representatives from each group—parents, educators, administrators, and others—in reaching a common understanding and in setting mutual goals.
2. *Examine the current practice.* Survey school staff, community leaders, and parents to ensure a clear understanding of the current status of parent and family involvement.
3. *Develop a plan of improvement.* Based on the evaluation of current practice, identify first steps and priority issues, including developing a parent/family involvement policy. Develop a comprehensive, well-balanced plan that includes activities related to each standard.
4. *Develop a written parent/family involvement policy.* A written policy establishes the vision, mission, and foundation for future plans.
5. *Secure support.* Keep stakeholders aware of the plan and its progress. Stakeholders include those responsible for implementation, those who will be affected, and those outside the school who may influence the outcome. Secure the financial resources needed.
6. *Provide professional development for school/program staff.* Effective training is essential. The best models of adult education provide staff and volunteers with several opportunities to explore the issues, work together, and monitor the evaluative progress.
7. *Evaluate and revise the plan.* Parent and family involvement is not a one-time goal. It merits a process of continuous improvement and commitment to long-term success.[19]

A number of school districts have worked hard at finding ways to bring about additional parental and family involvement in the schools. The Milwaukee City School District has developed a strategy that attempts to make the school building a true community center. Schools are used for adult literacy and technology training, social-service extended day programs, health services for the community, work force preparation programs, and early childhood classes. In addition, groups such as the Boy Scouts and the Brownies are encouraged to meet in their local school. "Male staff members and dads or significant males use the building for their monthly activities for the *Men are Talking* group." For all adult activities, childcare is provided.[20] By making the school the center of neighborhood activity, Milwaukee hopes to build a sense of community and to create positive feelings towards schools.

Trends in society have not made enlisting parental involvement in school any easier. Required background checks of volunteers can discourage some parents from becoming involved with their school. In Las Cruces, New Mexico, school authorities are requiring background checks and fingerprinting prior to allowing anyone to volunteer in a school. The fingerprinting costs the parents thirty-one dollars even if they are only agreeing to chaperone a field trip.[21] Although such security checks may be necessary, it would be hoped that public dollars might be used to defray the cost. With so much evidence of the positive value of parental participation, it would seem that schools should make every effort to encourage it.

Single parents and families in which both the mother and the father work full time create additional barriers to effective parental involvement. Special efforts have to be made to reach out to these families. For example, teacher–parent conference times must be flexible. Teachers should be willing to meet with parents occasionally outside the regular school day. The telephone can also be used effectively for parent–teacher discussions both before and after school. Additional special efforts must be made to communicate with low-income and non-English-speaking parents who are often afraid of contacting schools.[22]

Another facet of the challenge of increasing parental involvement is ensuring that school employees, from the superintendent to the custodians, are prepared to make parents feel welcomed and appreciated. Creating such an atmosphere in a school building might well require some faculty and staff training. Too many teachers are wary of parents who appear to be too interested in their children's education. These teachers need to be encouraged and instructed on how to maintain a healthy communication link with parents. This means more than sending out periodic progress reports and report cards. The goal must be to create a feeling of partnership between parents and teachers. Doing so can only enhance a child's academic progress.

Education critic Alfie Kohn has written that communication with parents can be improved if the conversations move beyond talking primarily about grades. He also advocates that teachers and parents sometimes involve students in their discussions. For him, the best way for parents to know what is happening with their child's education is to talk and listen to their own children.

> Children who aren't afraid of their parents' reaction, who are free of the pressures created by rewards (including praise) and punishments, feel safe to describe what excites them, bores them, angers them, and scares them about school. (Make a big deal about your kid's report card, one way or the other, and you'll probably be treated to less daily information about what your child is doing at school and how she feels about it.) Parents who show genuine, uncritical interest in what their children have figured out how to do are likely to be entrusted with the child's perspective on where she's succeeding and where she's struggling. But we have to trust and value that information rather than assuming we won't know what's really going on until we hear it from the teacher.[23]

Veteran teacher and administrator Deborah Meier also emphasizes the need for developing trust between school professionals and parents. She cautions teachers that developing such trust can be time consuming for any school personnel. In her book, *In Schools We Trust*, she quotes her own daughter who as a young teacher said that full-time teaching "was, by definition, an impossible job."[24] Teachers are pressed for time, and communication with parents often is a task that is only undertaken after other aspects of the teacher's work are done. To carry out the recommendations for involving parents contained in the *A Nation at Risk* report, most schools must place a higher priority on this issue and spend much more time and effort in attempting to increase parental involvement. Along with the special message to parents, the *A Nation at Risk* report includes a paragraph addressed to our nation's students. It is to this group that we turn next.

NOTES

1. U.S. Department of Education, The National Commission on Excellence in Education, *A Nation at Risk: The Imperative for Educational Reform*, April 1983, A Word to Parents and Students, 7.

2. U.S. Department of Education, *A Nation at Risk*, A Word to Parents and Students, 7.

3. San Diego County Office of Education, "Parent Involvement and Student Achievement," *Notes From Research*, www.sdcoe.k12.ca.us/notes/51/parstu.html (accessed 27 January 2004), 1.

4. San Diego County Office of Education, "Parent Involvement and Student Achievement," 3–6.

5. Diane Ravitch, *Left Back: A Century of Battles over School Reform* (New York: Simon & Schuster, 2000), 455.

6. Ravitch, *Left Back*, 455.

7. Pat Wingert, "I Do, I Do—Maybe," *Newsweek*, 2 November 1998; Karen S. Peterson, "Cohabitation Is Increasing, Census Data Confirm," *USA Today*, 13 August 2001, www.usatoday.com/news/census/2001-05-15-cohabitate.htm.

8. Stanley D. Eitzen, "Problem Students: The Sociological Roots," *Phi Delta Kappan*, April 1992, 584; David Francis, "New Figures Show Wider Gap Between Rich and Poor," *Christian Science Monitor*, 21 April 1995, 1, 8.

9. Myra Pollack Sadker and David Miller Sadker, *Teachers, Schools, and Society* (Boston: McGraw-Hill, 2003), 497.

10. Laurence Steinberg, *Beyond the Classroom* (New York: Simon & Schuster, 1996), 84.

11. Steinberg, *Beyond the Classroom*, 188.

12. Rebecca R. Kahlenberg, "Parents Skipping School," *National PTA*, www.pta.org/aboutpta/pressroom/innews12.asp (accessed 26 January 2004), 1.

13. Kathleen Cotton and Karen Reed Wikelund, "Parent Involvement in Education," *School Improvement Research*, www.nwrel.org/scpd/sirs/3/cu6.html (accessed 27 January 2004), 3–4.

14. Cotton and Wikelund, "Parent Involvement in Education," 6.

15. Cotton and Wikelund, "Parent Involvement in Education," 6.

16. Cotton and Wikelund, "Parent Involvement in Education," 6.

15. Cotton and Wikelund, "Parent Involvement in Education," 8.

17. Sue Miller Wiltz, "Bringing Parents on Board," *Harvard Education Letter* 20, no. 1 (January/February 2004): 2.

18. June Cavarretta, "Parents are a School's Best Friend," *Educational Leadership* 55, no. 8 (May 1998): 13.

19. Patricia Sullivan, "The PTA's National Standards," *Educational Leadership* 55, no. 8 (May 1998): 43–44.

20. Council of the Great City Schools, "Milwaukee Public Schools," www .cgcs.org/promise/parcomm.html (accessed 27 January 2004), 1.

21. Linda Jackson, "Volunteers Meet with Background Checks by Schools," *National PTA*, www.pta.org/aboutpta/pressroom/innews13.asp (accessed 26 January 2004), 1.

22. David C. Berliner and Bruce J. Biddle, *The Manufactured Crisis* (Reading, MA: Addison-Wesley Publishing, 1995), 195.

23. Alfie Kohn, *The Schools Our Children Deserve* (Boston: Houghton Mifflin Company, 1999), 195.

24. Deborah Meier, *In Schools We Trust* (Boston: Beacon Press, 2002), 55.

CHAPTER 12

The Students

Although it devotes only one paragraph to encouraging students, the authors of the *A Nation at Risk* report obviously saw the importance of having students who were highly motivated and excited about learning. Whether the *A Nation at Risk* report was ever read by many students, their inclusion in the report at least recognizes the fact that the students are part of our nation's educational problem. Veteran teachers and school administrators often talk about the fact that the children in their classrooms during the past two decades have been profoundly affected by television and the computer. In fact, some would say that the influence of this technology has been a significant factor in defining the unique characteristics of today's youth. Teachers who have taught for many years frequently comment that today's young people have a shortened attention span which they attribute in large part to the many hours students spend watching television and playing computer games. This, coupled with a quickened lifestyle, has made students today different and more difficult to teach than previous generations.

Laurence Steinberg and his associates spent ten years studying what they labeled student "engagement." They define this quality as time when students are able to "concentrate on the task"; when they "strive to do their best when tested or called upon"; and, "when they are given homework or other outside assignments, they do them on time and in good faith."[1] Because doing well in the classroom is an excellent predictor of later success, the challenge of bringing about student "engagement" is undoubtedly a significant factor if there is to be meaningful educational reform. The following results of the Steinberg study are quite alarming:

An extremely high proportion of American high school students did not take school, or their studies, seriously.

- Over one-third of the students we surveyed said that they get through the day in school primarily by "goofing off with their friends."
- Two-thirds of the students in our sample say they cheated on a school test during the past year. Nearly nine out of ten students in our sample say they copied someone else's homework sometime during the past year.

American students' time out of school is seldom spent in activities that reinforce what they are learning in their classes. More typically, their time and energy is focused on activities that compete with, rather than compliment, their studies.

- The average American high school student spends about four hours per week on homework outside of school. In other industrialized countries, the average is about four hours per *day*. Half of all the students in our study reported not doing the homework they are assigned. Fewer than 15 percent of students spend as much as five hours each week reading for pleasure. One-third say they spend five or more hours each week "partying" with their friends.
- Two-thirds of high school students are employed, and half hold down a part-time job that takes up more than fifteen hours weekly. One in six works more than twenty-five hours each week. More than one-third of students who work say they take easier classes so that their job won't hurt their grades.
- Nearly 40 percent of students who participate in a school-sponsored extracurricular activity, usually athletics, say they are often so tired from it that they can't study.

The adolescent peer culture in contemporary America demeans academic success and scorns students who try to do well in school. Schools are fighting a losing battle against a peer culture that disparages academic success.

- Fewer than one in five students say their friends think it is important to get good grades in school. Less than one-fourth of all students regularly discuss their schoolwork with their friends.

- When asked what crowd in school they would most like to be part of, nearly one-third said the "partiers," and nearly one-sixth said the "druggies." Only one in ten said the "brains."
- Nearly 20 percent of all students say they do not try as hard as they can in school because they are worried about what their friends might think.[2]

The above statistics are indeed disturbing, but it should not be assumed that the anti-achievement attitude of students is found equally in all schools. In many of our most highly achieving schools, most students do care deeply about their schoolwork. Too often, unfortunately, negative attitudes toward learning are found in schools containing our most disadvantaged children. Such schools are often located in urban and rural areas. The crux of the problem highlighted by Steinberg and others is that the proportions of disengaged students is increasing. "Two decades ago, a teacher in an average high school in this country could expect to have three or four 'difficult' students in a class of thirty. Today, teachers in these same schools are expected to teach to classrooms in which nearly half of the students have 'checked out.'"[3]

Television journalist John Merrow has commented on what he calls the "Anti-Youth Mood." He quotes researcher Meg Bostrom who has written that "only 15 percent of American adults believe that young people have a strong sense of right and wrong." In 1952, 52 percent of the adults surveyed believed that young people had this quality. The national press, including *Time*, *Newsweek*, *U.S News and World Report*, *People*, and *The National Inquirer*, all have featured cover articles that were critical of young people. In some of these stories our students were depicted as being antisocial, deprived, and dangerous.[4] There are many other people who have found reasons to criticize today's youth. Still, one must remember that adults have found reasons to be critical of young people during every historical era. The fact is that today's students also have their defenders.

Laura Sessions Stepp published a story in the *Washington Post* which included a number of what she considered prevailing myths concerning adolescents in our society. These myths (and some contradictory facts) include the following:

1. *Adolescents yearn to be independent of adults, particularly their parents, and we must let go of them so they can establish autonomy.* Only a minority of teenagers engage in serious rebellion against their parents. A number of surveys have shown that most young people want closer contact with adults, including their parents. A large majority of the teenagers surveyed believe that their parents are "supportive and caring."

2. *Adolescents are dangerous.* The fact is that adults are responsible for three-fourths of the increase in violent crime. Juvenile crime has been declining for the past six years and it has declined more quickly than adult crime.

3. *Adolescents don't need regular health care because, in general, they are pretty healthy.* The health of young people is not what it could be. There is an increase in asthma as well as a serious problem with overweight young people. On the other hand, adolescents seem to be making better decisions with regard to the use of drugs and alcohol. Teen deaths from drunk driving accidents have declined 59 percent since 1982.

4. *Adolescents are lazy and irresponsible.* More teenagers are staying in school longer and many are becoming involved in service projects in their community. Each year more students take challenging college courses during their high school years.

5. *Adolescents are merely "raging hormones" walking around thinking about sex every waking hour of the day.* To their credit, fewer teens are getting pregnant.

6. *Adolescents are negatively influenced by their peers.* Although teenagers do look to their friends in matters such as dress, music and language, they continue to be influenced greatly by their parents and other adults. At the same time peer influence can be beneficial to a young person's self-esteem and desire for achievement.[5]

An article published in *Educational Leadership* also cites some statistics in defense of today's students. For example, of the 52 million students in U.S. schools, approximately twenty-four are murdered in school each year. At the same time, it is estimated that as many as 3,000 kids are murdered by their parents in the same time period.[6]

In his book, *Choosing Excellence*, John Merrow concludes a chapter entitled "Our Kids are Not the Problem" with these words:

> Children and adolescents need and want adult guidance, support and companionship. As the number of children increases from 70 million in 1999 to a projected 77.6 million in 2020, we cannot continue to disinvest in young people, turn our backs on them, and dismiss them as "dangerous" or worse. That's not only a self-fulfilling prophecy; it's also a sure-fire recipe for social disaster.[7]

While the debate about American youth will be ongoing, there are changes in the makeup of the student bodies of our schools that must be taken into account when we consider any reforms of public education:

- By 2012, the West (the geographic area expected to witness the greatest changes) will become "minority majority," with no single racial or ethnic group having a majority.
- The nation has approximately 2.5 million Native Americans, a number that increases to about 4 million when including Americans claiming partial Indian heritage on the census.
- By 2000, the number of Asians, including Asian Indians, in the United States was over 10 million or 3.6 percent of the population.
- About 6 million Americans claimed multi-racial heritage with 2 or more races indicated on Census 2000.
- By 2030, the number of U.S. residents who are non-white or Hispanic will be about 140 million or about 40 percent of the U.S. population.[8]

Although the number of non-Caucasians in our schools will continue to grow, we must face the reality that, except for Asian Americans, this is the group that is doing the least well academically. The *A Nation at Risk* report did focus on the need to give additional assistance to minorities and other disadvantaged youth. Unfortunately, if Jeff Howard is correct in his assessment contained in the book *A Nation Reformed?*, the results of these efforts have been "disappointing." He notes that in the year 2000, 88 percent of the African American children tested in the National Assessment of Education Progress "failed to reach a level of reading required to fully decode the increasingly complex material that they will encounter in their textbooks." For Hispanic children, the situation is "almost as dismal." It is true that scores on some standardized examinations have improved, however our student achievement problem in most urban areas remains monumental. Howard concludes that "twenty years after the publication of the *A Nation at Risk* report we had a right to expect something better."[9]

If indeed we are making too little progress with disadvantaged youth, it is important to ask what we can do in the United States to help these young people. The *A Nation at Risk* report and the resulting state curriculum standards, high-stakes testing, and accountability have been the major initiatives to improve academic learning. It would seem that at least in the eyes of current high school students many schools have failed to "live up to all the 'striving for excellence' mottoes that have popped up in all those school lobbies since the publication of *A Nation at Risk*." In one survey conducted by Public Agenda, half the students surveyed said that their schools "didn't challenge them to do their best." Another poll of secondary students found 70 percent saying that they were doing "the minimum they need to get by."[10]

While many students are apparently not overly extending themselves in their high school classes, two-thirds of 4,000 high school students surveyed in 2003 "agreed that their schools had prepared them for college as well as any school in the country." Even a majority of the African American and Hispanic students agreed with the statement.[11] These responses might also say something about the expectations of our institutions of higher learning. Whether it is lower expectations by our colleges or poor high school training, it would appear that we need to find better ways to challenge and motivate our teenagers to work harder on their schoolwork.

Laurence Steinberg has a number of suggestions:

- *Make school performance really count.* This means that we must reward excellence and punish failure. Parents, employers and colleges should demand better academic performance. Unless they do, students will continue to just slide by.
- *Adopt a system of national standards and examinations.* We cannot continue to have the great variety of academic standards from one state to another. "Individual districts might be free to set higher standards than those mandated, but all should be expected to comply with national minimums."

- *Develop uniform national standards for school transcripts.* "One reason that actual school performance matters so little is that we have no standardized way of communicating information about a student's academic accomplishments to parents, employers, and educators. . . . Standardized school transcripts should be developed that provide information about student performance on national achievement examinations, courses completed (with some indication of course difficulty), grades earned, and other indicators of scholastic motivation, such as school attendance."
- *Eliminate remedial education at 4-year colleges and universities.* Providing this kind of education trivializes the high school diploma and diminishes "the meaning of college admission." Such remedial work, if it is at all necessary after high school, should be done at local community colleges prior to a student's admission to a more advanced institution of higher learning.
- *Support appropriate school-sponsored extracurricular activities.* Schools should reexamine their extracurricular programs to ensure that they do not tax students' time and energy unnecessarily. Athletic programs, particularly football and basketball, warrant special scrutiny, since these are activities that tend to be the most time-consuming.
- *Limit youngsters' time in after-school jobs.* Students who are employed more than twenty hours a week perform more poorly than their peers academically. They are less committed to their education and less engaged in class compared with their classmates. It is possible for a state to limit the number of hours which high school students can legally work.[12]

Many of these solutions as well as others that have been suggested to increase student motivation will require significant changes in the way schools operate. Whether it be programs involving students, parents, administrators, or teachers, it is fair to say that many of the options will have financial implications for our schools. To realistically expect to reform American education, especially for our disadvantaged students, one must give serious consideration to our current method of financing schools and to what the options are if we wish to improve upon the present system.

NOTES

1. Laurence Steinberg, *Beyond the Classroom* (New York: Simon & Schuster, 1996), 15.

2. Steinberg, *Beyond the Classroom*, 18–19.

3. Steinberg, *Beyond the Classroom*, 28.

4. John Merrow, *Choosing Excellence* (Lanham, MD: Scarecrow Press, 2001), 116–117.

5. Merrow, *Choosing Excellence*, 121–23.

6. Carol Tell, "Generation What?" *Educational Leadership* 57, no. 4 (December 1999): 8–9.

7. Merrow, *Choosing Excellence*, 124.

8. Myra Pollack Sadker and David Miller Sadker, *Teachers, Schools, and Society* (Boston: McGraw-Hill, 2003), 47–48.

9. David T. Gordon, ed., *A Nation Reformed?* (Cambridge, MA: Harvard Education Press, 2003), 82.

10. Bess Keller, "Less Than Awesome," *Education Week*, 23 April 2003, http://www.edweek.org/ew/ewstory.cfm?slug=32youth.h22 (accessed 16 December 2003), 4.

11. Keller, "Less Than Awesome," 3–4.

12. Steinberg, *Beyond the Classroom*, 191–93.

CHAPTER 13

The Money

Although the *A Nation at Risk* report does not recommend major changes in the funding of education, many of the reforms that it advocates would necessitate new investments in our schools. Several examples of recommendations that would probably be costly are listed below.

- The introduction of new standardized tests.
- Consideration of a 200–220 day school year (teachers' unions would undoubtedly demand significant salary increases for such a concession regarding their work calendar). Included also is a recommendation for eleven-month contracts for teachers. This too would be an extremely expensive reform.
- Grants and loans for outstanding individuals entering the teaching profession.
- An overall increase in teacher salaries to make them "professionally competitive."
- Increased professional development opportunities for teachers.
- Federal government assistance for "collecting data, . . . supporting curriculum improvement and research on teaching, learning, and the management of schools."
- Federal government should provide assistance to schools for meeting the "needs of key groups of students such as the gifted and talented, socioeconomically disadvantaged, minority and language minority students, and the handicapped."[1]

The specific recommendations dealing with responsibilities of the federal government were made even though the Reagan administration, which supposedly sponsored the report, was publicly supporting the abolition of a separate federal Department of Education. The conservative leaders within the administration strongly believed that education was primarily the responsibility of state governments and local school districts. Currently state governments provide approximately 48 percent of the funding for public schools, while 42 percent comes from local sources.[2] As noted earlier, President Lyndon B. Johnson and the Democratic Party moved the federal government into the field of public education as part of the War on Poverty. Still, the reality of educational funding in the United States as we entered the twenty-first century was that Washington was paying only about 7 percent of the cost of educating our nation's children. Although percentages vary from district to district, it is the state and local school districts that provide the primary sources of revenue for our schools.

At the state level, the money is raised by a variety of taxes. Most states rely primarily on a state income tax, but the sales tax is also a major source of revenue in many states. In some states, specific revenue sources have been assigned to the schools. New York State for instance distributes the profits from its statewide lottery directly to public school districts. Currently the state legislature in New York is considering the use of revenues from state-sponsored gambling operations to help finance schools. Despite a number of critics of the practice of state sponsorship of gambling, it would seem that legislators are willing to use almost any method to raise money for schools.

Historically, in most areas it has been the property tax levied by the local school district that has provided the primary local revenues for schools. This tax has the advantage that it can be effectively administered at the local level. It also has an enforcement tool that ensures most often that the tax will be paid since the ultimate penalty for nonpayment is the loss of the owner's property.

On the other hand, the property tax has a number of significant problems as a source of revenue. To begin with, it is a difficult tax to administer fairly. Local assessors have the almost impossible task of maintaining accurate records on the value of each piece of property in their communities. Most often there is an attempt made to peg the assessment to the probable selling price of a property at that moment in time. To do so, the assessor must use the selling price of similar properties in that area.

In addition, the assessor must attempt to be aware of improvements made in a home or a business that might increase its value. Realizing the difficulty of keeping up-to-date assessment rolls, some states have attempted to measure the accuracy of each local assessor and assign an "equalization rate" that is designed to ensure fairness in an inexact system.

Along with the fairness issue, property taxes do affect some members of a community more than others. Because they are not tied to the income of local residents, property owners who have a fixed income will have problems keeping up with an ever-increasing school tax rate. The group affected most by the issue of fixed incomes is senior citizens who rely on pension payments that remain the same each year. While senior citizens' primary income remains constant, school taxes continue to increase, and in many areas the increase has been in excess of the inflation rate. As a result, some seniors have faced serious problems in continuing to pay their school taxes. The problem is made worse by the fact that they are also paying property taxes to their town, village, and county governments.

Another group that can be hurt by property taxes are farmers. Depending on the year, a farmer's income can be very different. Because they often own large tracts of land which might have numerous buildings, farmers are likely to have a large property-tax bill even if they had not had a profitable year. Small businesses can also face similar problems.

Governments also grant exemptions for many types of property. Churches, all government facilities, and nonprofit organizations are not responsible for paying property taxes. Sometimes local communities offer reductions in property taxes to veterans. A school district that has a military base or Native American reservation will be responsible for the children from these areas but will not be allowed to collect property taxes.

These problems can all be affected by laws that attempt to make the system fairer. Additional reductions in property taxes can be and are often made for senior citizens with limited income, farmers, and especially new businesses beginning in a community. The single largest difficulty with the property tax as a primary source of income for schools is its unevenness as a revenue source.

School districts with large, valuable businesses or very high residential property values will be better able to raise large amounts of money with a property tax. A community with houses that have an average assessment of $300,000 will be able to raise three times as much money with a tax rate of $20 per thousand as will a district that has an average assessment of $100,000. In some rural and urban communities, the average assessed value of a home is considerably less than $100,000, and such school districts find it hard to assess property taxes on their residents whose income is considerably lower than that of the residents of nearby affluent suburbs. Thus the property wealth of a district becomes the primary factor in determining how easy it will be to raise local funds for public education. The result of the reliance on property taxes is that our wealthy suburban districts are frequently able to spend several times as much per pupil as a poor district. This discrepancy in taxing potential is supposed to be made up by the state government. In theory, the state government will give more money to property-poor districts than to wealthy districts. Most states make an effort to do so, and poor districts do receive a larger percentage of their income from the state. The political reality of the system, though, is that in a number of states less affluent districts continue to have much less to spend per pupil than do richer communities.

Attempts to remedy such situations are made difficult by the political power of suburban legislators. Because their constituents constantly pressure them to keep state aid payments coming, these representatives oppose any change that would have a negative effect on state aid to the schools in their district. Despite the fact that some school districts are able to spend three or even four times as much per pupil as poorer districts, too many states have done little to remedy the situation. Even with public "wake up calls" with such books as Jonathan Kozol's *Savage Inequalities*, the system has not responded. The only exception has been a recent series of state court decisions that have attempted to force state governments to do a better job of providing equality of educational opportunity to the children of their state.

Beginning in 1973 with the U.S Supreme Court decision in *Rodriguez v. San Antonio*, there have been thirty state supreme court cases that have challenged the ways schools have been financed in their states. The cases have been concerned primarily with charges of discrimination based on race or social class. Although many are aimed at the inequalities caused by unequal property tax bases, some also attack "bizarre funding formulas that dispense state aid in ways that perpetuate inequality." To some critics, these cases also seek to fight against general government policies that are "preserving pockets of privilege" and moving away from "civil rights era concerns for equity, desegregation, and social justice." To those who are opposed to the current funding mechanisms, they are in part responsible for a "growing economic stratification in society at large."[3]

Up to now, slightly less than half of the thirty cases have been decided in favor of those challenging the education aid formulas in their state. Even when the state governments lost these cases, reform has not been swift. For example, in New Jersey the formula has been declared inadequate in various ways no less than nine times but the state government has yet to devise an equitable funding formula to meet the demands of the court. The legal history in this area would show that

> court decisions, in themselves, have been insufficient to ensure equity for several reasons. While glaring disparities in school funding have occasionally persuaded Courts to order reform, it has been almost impossible to prevent Governors and state legislators from evading or limiting the impact of the court orders. Restrained by separation-of-powers concerns and the prevailing conservative political climate, Courts have generally given states wide latitude to proceed with the half-measures and "good faith" efforts, sometimes promising further review if they prove inadequate.[4]

In New York State, the highest court has ordered the state government to revise its state aid formula to ensure that the students in New York City are receiving an equal educational opportunity with other students in the state. A commission appointed by governor George Pataki has concluded that the state must provide an additional seven billion dollars to satisfy the court order. Currently the state is budgeting a total of fourteen billion for public schools. Even more alarming is the assertion by the commission that "more than five hundred of the seven hundred public school districts in the state are not receiving sufficient aid to meet the constitutional imperative of providing a 'sound, basic education.'" An editorial in the Rochester, New York *Democrat and Chronicle* puts the blame on a number of factors including "fat bureaucracies, weak administrators and school boards, ill-prepared teachers, and detached or even alienated parents."[5]

Despite such opinions, public support for additional funding for education remains strong. In Maryland, where the state legislature had promised to increase education expenditures and failed to do so, thousands of teachers, parents, and students from across the state rallied in Annapolis in an effort to seek additional funding for schools. The rally participants also criticized the governor's plan to tie school funding to an initiative to allow the introduction of slot machines in the state.[6]

Even if states could develop formulas that provided an equal per-pupil payment for every student in the state, the arguments would continue. Wealthy communities would charge that they have to spend more on teacher salaries because of the cost of living in their district. This would be primarily true for teachers who seek to live in a wealthy residential community where real-estate costs are high. On the other hand, there are those who suggest that poorer districts need to spend more per pupil because of the educational needs of their students. Such schools might have a higher percentage of special education students as well as a large number of children with limited English proficiency. It is also true that the school buildings in poor districts have become outdated and are in need of repair or replacement. Jonathan Kozol illustrated the problem when he wrote that "equity, after all, does not mean simply equal funding. Equal funding for unequal needs is not equality."[7]

> Years of racial segregation and unequal funding have resulted in schools that are dilapidated and even dangerous for students. Teachers in Chicago's inner cities make do with popcorn poppers as Bunsen burners, plastic pop bottles are laboratory dishes, and work with 15-year-old textbooks, if they even have enough for the whole class. James D. Squires, a former editor of the *Chicago Tribune*, wrote that "it took an extraordinary combination of greed, racism, political cowardice and public apathy to let the public schools in Chicago get so bad."[8]

Even with such disparities, there are many who continue to suggest that more money will make little difference in the quality of our schools. Typical of this point of view is an article in the *Wall Street Journal* written by Jay P. Greene. Writing about the New York City schools, he points out that the school district was spending more than $10,000 annually per student, which placed New York in the top 5 percent for city school spending in the entire United States. He went on to note that nationally, real per-pupil spending during the past thirty years has doubled, while test scores have not greatly improved. Greene compares spending money on schools to giving funds to a "drunk panhandler. . . . It may make the giver feel better but it does not change the drunk's life."[9]

More objective data comes from researchers who have compared educational spending in the United States with other nations. The Organization for Economic Cooperation and Development has concluded that "countries that spend more are countries that do better," but others would say that the United States is an exception to this rule. An outspoken critic of public education spending, Chester E. Finn Jr. believes that lower test scores have been caused by "educationists," primarily education professors and bureaucrats. He has written that "the lunatics have taken over the asylum."[10]

The conservative Heritage Foundation has also weighed in on the money question. In an article entitled "Why More Money Will Not Solve America's Educational Crisis," Kirk A. Johnson and Krista Kafer asked the reader to consider the following information:

- Total expenditures by the U.S. Department of Education for all K–12 students have nearly doubled, in constant dollars, just since the 1980s, from $14.8 billion to $27.1 billion; but
- Reading and math scores on the National Assessment of Educational Progress (NAEP) have changed relatively little over the same period, despite the enormous increases in spending at the federal, state, and local levels.[11]

The authors go on to point to the work of the National Research Council, which summed up its findings in a report in 1999 commissioned by the U.S. Department of Education. It concluded that "additional funding for education will not automatically and necessarily generate student achievement and in the past has not, in fact, generally led to higher student achievement. The fact that some 68 percent of fourth graders could not read at a proficient level on the NAEP exam last year reinforces this conclusion."[12] Based on these findings, Johnson and Kafer strongly suggest that the only way to solve our educational problems is to institute a true choice system in the field of education.

Rather than bolster funding for programs that have failed to increase student achievement, House and Senate conferees on the reauthorization of the Elementary and Secondary Education Act should target funding to results-oriented approaches, such as the President's proposal to establish charter states and school choice initiatives. Federal money should go toward real reforms that boost achievement.[13]

Those who argue that we must increase our investment in education point out that a significant number of programs that had been financed by additional government spending were not directly linked to improving test scores, especially such tests as the college entrance examination known as the Scholastic Assessment Test. Thirty percent of the new money has been spent on improving special education. Many of these students who have participated in special education programs will never take the SAT or many of the other examinations that are being given to monitor academic success. Ten percent of the new money spent by the federal government in recent years has gone to school lunch and breakfast programs, while 5 percent has gone to school transportation and 3 percent to dropout prevention. None of this money directly affected test scores, although such expenditures have helped to reduce the dropout rate from 12.2 percent in 1970 to 9.2 percent in the 1990s.[14]

Whether or not one accepts the idea that additional overall expenditures for education will be helpful in improving academic achievement, it remains true that spending for public schools both within a state and between states remains significantly unequal. There are school districts that are spending three or four times more per pupil than other districts. Given the magnitude of these differences, it would seem that this remains an issue that must be addressed. One alternative is to spend billions of dollars to bring expenditures for students in poor districts up to what is being spent in wealthy districts. A second approach would be to redistribute the money by reducing state aid to wealthy districts and giving the money to communities with a small property-tax base. Politically, neither alternative is likely to be embraced by elected officials. Realizing this, some courts have used another measure for gauging the acceptability of state funding formulas. For these judges, the test has become "adequacy." Instead of seeking equality of opportunity for all students, some courts are now saying that funding must be adequate to meet a level of excellence necessary for a student to have a fair chance of succeeding in that school district. Even with "adequacy" as the goal, the commission in New York State concluded that five hundred of the seven hundred school districts were unable to meet the state constitutional requirement of giving students "a sound, basic education."[15]

New York is not unique in facing this type of problem, and because of our historic commitment to local control of schools, it is extremely difficult to change the current system. Even if one were to suggest a complete overhaul of the way we finance schools, the economic conditions in the United States at this time are not conducive to changing the system. In many countries it is the national government that provides funding for schools. Because of the huge deficit in the federal budget and the need to fund our current war on terrorism, it is not likely that the government in Washington will even consider increasing federal aid to schools dramatically.

Many states also have a deficit problem that will make it difficult to appropriate additional money for education. The only exception is likely to be in those states where courts are pushing the legislatures to upgrade their financial aid to poor districts. Finally, it is also true that most local governments have pushed their property tax rates about as high as their communities will accept. It is possible that an increase in the sales tax in a state could be a new source of income, but this is never a popular alternative. Many states have already placed new taxes on items such as tobacco, alcohol products, and gasoline. The fact that some states are resorting more and more to gambling receipts suggests that there are not too many sources of new money that haven't been tapped. As a result, despite its many shortcomings, it is not likely that the property tax will soon disappear as a primary source of income for schools. The one positive gleam of hope is that the American public continues to place a very high priority on improving schools. Most voters probably would support a higher state income tax especially if it was placed on the wealthy. Others would not mind additional taxes on corporate profits. This source is probably not going to be utilized because communities and states are now competing with each other for new businesses.

In many communities, there are outspoken individuals who say what we need to do is to "cut the fat" out of our school budgets. For many, this means reducing administrative costs and managing our schools more effectively. This line of thinking leads local critics to seek to reduce the non-teaching personnel employed in their schools. District administrators point to the dramatic increases in paperwork mandated by the federal and state governments and suggest that these mandates have made it necessary to create more non-teaching jobs in our schools.

They also argue that the ratio between managers and workers in schools is much higher than in most private firms. A school principal could very well be responsible for supervising fifty faculty members, fifteen non-teaching personnel, and eight hundred students. In any case, whenever money becomes less plentiful, non-teaching positions in schools do disappear along with teachers and programs that are not required by the state. Unfortunately, it is the poorer schools that have less possible cuts to consider than wealthier districts.

Although it is not accepted by a majority of the people in the United States, it is likely that the federal government has the best chance of providing the necessary funds to significantly reduce the discrepancies in spending from one state to another. There are undoubtedly some states that have the necessary resources to increase their financial commitment to education, but because of economic conditions, there are other states where this would be more difficult. Leaving the primary funding of education to state and local governments has produced the current inequitable situation. It is possible that the courts in most states will force changes, but it is hard to be optimistic about the near future. In the words of Timothy A. Hacsi:

Even if the evidence were to become crystal clear about how to build superb schools in every school district, it would be an extraordinarily difficult thing to do, in part because the financing of schools would remain, fundamentally, a political issue. To increase school budgets, taxes have to be increased somewhere; should they be local property taxes, or state sales or income taxes, or should the federal government greatly increase its contribution? How can the public—most of which does not have children of school age—be convinced that more money should go to schools rather than their own more direct needs? Perhaps the first step is wider recognition by politicians and citizens that, while money will not automatically make a difference, it is a necessary component of any true educational reform, especially when it comes to our most troubled schools.[16]

Financing our schools is likely to remain a major issue at all levels of government. Of all the factors that might affect this extremely complex problem, there is one that was not specifically addressed in the *A Nation at Risk* report. This is true even though the Republican Party had already embraced the concept at the time of the study. The campaign to institute a program allowing for school choice has been with us since even before 1983, and it remains a divisive and controversial issue in the first decade of the twenty-first century.

NOTES

1. U.S. Department of Education, The National Commission on Excellence in Education, *A Nation at Risk: The Imperative for Educational Reform*, April 1983, Recommendations, 4–6.

2. U.S. Department of Education, National Center for Education Statistics, "Statistics of State School Systems; Revenues and Expenditures for Public Elementary and Secondary Education; and Common Core of Data Surveys," *Digest of Education Statistics* (2001, 2002): table 158.

3. Stan Karp, "Money, Schools, and Courts," *Z Magazine*, December 1995, www.geocities.com/Athens/Cyprus/6547/money.html (accessed 6 February 2004).

4. Karp, "Money, Schools, and Courts," 2.

5. *Democrat and Chronicle*, "More than Money," 6 February 2004, sec. A, p. 10.

6. Nancy Trejos and Vikki Ortiz, "Thornton Plan Funding Demanded," *Washington Post*, 10 February 2004, www.washingtonpost.com/wp-dyn/articles/A26938-2004Feb9.html (accessed 13 February 2004), 1–2.

7. LeeAnn Brooks, "School Financing: America's Caste System," *Education 396, School and Society*, http://t3.preservice.org/T0110780/poverty%20web.htm (accessed 6 February 2004), 3.

8. Brooks, "School Financing," 3.

9. Jay P. Greene, "Raise Standards, Not Money," *The Wall Street Journal*, 7 October 2002, www.manhattan-institute.org/html/_wsj-raise_standards.htm (accessed 6 February 2004).

10. Suzanne Fields, "Throwing Money at the Schoolhouse Frauds," *Townhall* 22, September 2003, www.townhall.com/columnists/suzannefields/sf20030922.shtml (accessed 6 February 2004), 2.

11. Kirk A. Johnson and Krista Kafer, "Why More Money Will Not Solve America's Education Crisis," *The Heritage Foundation*, 11 June 2001, www.heritage.org/Research/Education/BG1448.cfm (accessed 6 February 2004), 1.

12. Johnson, "Why More Money Will Not Solve America's Education Crisis," 5.

13. Johnson, "Why More Money Will Not Solve America's Education Crisis," 9.

14. Steve Kangas, "Doubling the Money Spent on Education Hasn't Improved It," www.huppi.com/kangaroo/L-edumoney.htm (accessed 6 February 2004), 1.

15. *Democrat and Chronicle*, "More than Money," sec. A., p. 10.

16. Timothy A. Hacsi, *Children as Pawns* (Cambridge, MA: Harvard University Press, 2002), 203.

CHAPTER 14

The Choice

The idea of giving parents and students a choice of schools has been discussed in the United States for fifty years. Many educational historians trace the concept to the suggestion of economist Milton Friedman to establish a school voucher system.[1] Friedman and others have argued that public schools have had a virtual monopoly in enrolling most of the students in the United States. Although there have also been private schools, they have not been a realistic option for families who could not pay the tuition. Because of the lack of competition, advocates of choice believe that there has been little motivation for public schools to improve. Instead they have become bloated with administrators, bogged down in regulations, and, according to some, controlled by teachers' unions. The argument for choice goes on to suggest that by utilizing the very American concept of free enterprise and competition, schools would have to perform well or eventually go out of business. For those who support school choice, it allows parents to become consumers who would carefully seek the best possible school for their children. Having done this, both parents and students would be more likely to be committed to a school that they have selected.

Although the idea of choice is not a new idea, it has gained momentum slowly in the United States. There are some parents who have rejected all schools for their children. Homeschooling is an alternative that is growing. Parents, motivated by a desire to provide a safer and less threatening environment, along with many others who are committed to teaching their own religious views, have chosen to teach their children at home. As a result, a number of organizations have created curriculum materials for homeschoolers, and statewide and national organizations have been formed. Most of these groups represent a conservative Christian perspective. While twenty years ago there were only 12,500 students being homeschooled, current estimates range as high as a million and a half. Critics of the practice have pointed out that children educated at home will lack social interaction with children and adults who might be different from themselves. In other words, it has been suggested that the children are being sheltered from the "real world." Others have pointed to the fact that some parents who have chosen to teach their own children lack the necessary training and knowledge, especially for teaching students advanced courses at the secondary level. Realizing some of the limitations, homeschool parents in many areas have banded together to provide a variety of social and academic opportunities for their children. It is not unusual for such groups to sponsor special classes in music, art, and physical education, or even to organize competitive athletic teams. Many homeschool parents also have learned to broaden their children's educational opportunities by using programs available on computers. While most parents who homeschool are not trained teachers, "individualized instruction is powerful. This may be one reason homeschooled children generally score quite well on standardized tests, averaging between the sixty-fifth and ninetieth percentiles."[2]

Although the number of families choosing to teach their children at home continues to grow slowly, especially with elementary age students, social and economic realities in the United States will limit the number of parents who choose this option. Since the majority of parents now hold full-time jobs, those families seeking an educational choice must look to other alternatives.

The earliest widespread movement that allowed some parents and students to choose a school other than the one in their neighborhood came at the same time as the civil rights movement in the 1960s and 1970s. Magnet schools have been defined as schools "offering specialized and unique programs designed to attract students from throughout the district."[3] The idea was that magnet schools would break down segregation within a district. For example, an African American student would be able to travel across the city if he or she was interested in enrolling in a magnet school for the arts. At the same time, a student from an area dominated by Hispanics might give up attendance at a neighborhood high school to attend a vocational school in another part of the city.[4] While desegregation was one of the reasons for establishing magnet schools, perhaps even more important was that magnet schools became the first important example of school choice. The idea of magnet schools has caught on. By the year 2000, thirty-three states were reporting data regarding magnet schools. Nationwide, there were 1,372 magnet schools, with the most being in California and Illinois.[5]

Located primarily in large districts, magnet schools each have a specific curriculum focus. A magnet school could be designed for honors students, vocational students, or those with a special interest in science or the arts. At the elementary level, a Montessori school could become a magnet school for very young children. These schools all have the same regulations as other public schools and are governed by state law and the local board of education. Students must meet all of the curriculum requirements prescribed by their state. Faculty members of magnet schools must have state certification, and they are represented by the same union as other teachers working in the district. What would be different is that at a magnet school, such as one focusing on the arts, there would be an attempt to build an outstanding art and music program for those students who chose this option. These students would have to seek acceptance at the school by preparing an art portfolio or participating in an audition. The school district would likely spend additional funds on the arts for this school, and along with the regular state mandated courses, there would be a number of electives in art and music not offered in other schools. Like any plan allowing school choice, there are arguments both for and against magnet schools. The Education Commission of the States has summarized the arguments as follows:

Pros
- When schools, such as magnets, offer specialized curriculum programs that emphasize a consistent theme or method of teaching, they facilitate student and teacher commitment to the school.
- Because magnet schools often attract students from outside the neighborhood surrounding the school, they encourage the voluntary integration of public schools.
- Magnet schools increase the choices available to parents and students in urban school districts.

Cons
 • Low-income, English-as-a-second language [*sic*] and special education students are underrepresented in magnets.
 • The selective admissions criteria of magnet schools create firewalls for students with failing grades or records of bad behavior or truancy who want to attend these schools.
 • Many magnet schools may be drawing scarce energy and resources away from improving neighborhood schools.[6]

While the idea of magnet schools continues to be quite popular in many cities, it is less practical in rural areas and smaller suburbs. In any school district, transportation remains a problem for school choice programs. This is especially true in rural areas where the nearest alternative school might be located miles away from a student's home. In any case, alternatives other than having students attend their neighborhood schools create a difficult decision for a local board of education. If it becomes the parent's responsibility to transport their children to their school of choice, such a plan restricts families that are unable to provide transportation. On the other hand, if the district assumes the cost for transporting students, it can be both confusing and expensive. Because of some of these limitations, the practice of establishing new magnet schools may not become a widespread option in the years ahead.

Another plan that has been adopted by some public school districts is a policy known as open enrollment. This concept allows students some choice in selecting another public school within the district or, in some cases, among neighboring districts. "Since 1988, eighteen states have enacted legislation allowing transfer both within and among school districts. Another eleven states have regulations allowing transfer only within the same district. Nearly 4 million students participate in open-enrollment programs."[7] Even though open-enrollment options create the same transportation options as other choice plans, they do provide flexibility for parents who are unhappy with their neighborhood school.

During the first decade of this century, the choice plan that currently is growing most rapidly is the establishment of so-called charter schools. One textbook defines a charter school as being an independent public school "supported by state funds but freed from many regulations and run by individuals who generally have the power to hire and to fire colleagues and to budget money as they see fit."[8] The idea is that any individual or group may make an application to the state education department and to their local school district to begin a school that will be funded at the same per-pupil rate as other comparable schools in the district. Most states have limited the number of charter schools that may be approved. If the application is accepted, the new school is given a charter or contract to operate for a specific length of time, after which it must reapply to renew the charter. To be accepted, a charter application must convince the appropriate authorities that its plan for the school is educationally sound and that there are acceptable assessment methods. Although the laws from state to state vary, charter schools currently cannot be sponsored by churches, and they are required to follow the same guidelines relating to church and state as other public schools.

Charter schools must be open to all students in the district, and if they receive more applications than they have openings, students are most often selected by using a lottery. For supporters of charter schools, the primary advantage is that they are freed from almost all of the bureaucratic mandates faced by other public schools. A charter school has much more latitude in hiring teachers and administrators. In most states, teachers or administrators do not have to be certified, nor do they have to be members of the local teachers' union. In addition, charter schools are not required to offer tenure, and their employees may not be covered by the same fringe benefits as other individuals working in the district. The lengths of the school day and year are left to the individual governing body of the school. These schools often have more freedom as to the assessments that are used to measure student achievement. Their budgets are controlled almost totally at the school level, where a committee of parents, teachers, and the administrator make most of the important decisions. Like many magnet schools, individual charter schools often have a particular focus. Frequently, the primary role is to raise academic achievement by emphasizing a "back to basics" approach.

The late president of the American Federation of Teachers, Albert Shanker, "launched the charter school movement in a 1988 speech, when he suggested that teachers be empowered in charter schools, special schools that focus on student achievement."[9] The first charter school law was passed in Minnesota in 1991. Currently, thirty-eight states allow the formation of charter schools, and it is estimated that there are 2,500 such schools.[10] In recent years, a number of charters have been granted to private for-profit organizations such as the Edison Project. It is likely that the number of such organizations, which are called educational maintenance organizations, will grow and that the percentage of for-profit charter schools will increase. This trend has tended to create some additional concern about the growth of the charter school movement. There are those who have difficulty accepting that schools should be profit-making organizations.

In the way of a summary, one author has stated that "charter schools, in effect 'swap' rules and regulations for greater freedom and the promise that they will achieve better results." The following list of characteristics is typical of charter schools throughout the nation:

- Allows for the creation of a new or the conversion of an existing public school
- Prohibits admissions tests
- Is nonsectarian
- Requires a demonstrable improvement in performance
- Can be closed if it does not meet expectations
- Does not need to conform to most state rules and regulations
- Receives funding based on the number of students enrolled[11]

Like other forms of choice, there is still a lack of conclusive evidence on the overall achievement of students in charter schools. Still, attempts have been made to judge their success. Both liberal educator Theodore Sizer and conservative educational historian Diane Ravitch have suggested that the media has not done a good job of reporting on charter schools because "they've been looked upon as a coherent entity," which they are not.[12] Ravitch agreed with Sizer when she wrote, "I think reporters have a hard time understanding that there is a tremendous variety of charter schools. . . . You can pick a charter school that is very progressive or very 'back-to-basics' and then everything in between."[13]

One finds a variety of studies and expert opinions on the success of charter schools. A popular textbook on educational issues includes the following excerpt:

In the early 1990s, researchers concluded that despite positive benefits children who participate in charter schools received, little evidence directly connected these programs with improvement in school performance or student achievement. More recent studies, though, conclude that in some cases, the presence of even this limited form of competition causes school districts to improve their services. For example, in New York City, District 4, where parents had choices about the schools their children would attend, math and reading test scores improved more than in any of the other thirty-two community districts.[14]

Another author, Susan H. Fuhrman, concluded that there is "little evidence" that charter schools "lead to improved achievement or greater instructional innovation." On the other hand, the same author admits that "charters rank high in parental satisfaction and involvement."[15] Because of their popularity with parents, it is likely that state and local governments will continue to approve of the formation of new charter schools.

Although there has been fairly wide support of charter schools, the concept of school vouchers has always been more controversial. This is especially true when the plan allows the vouchers to be used for private religious schools. As noted earlier, the idea of voucher plans has been discussed for half of a century. During that time, several variations of the idea have emerged. They include the following:

Universal vouchers

Allowing all parents to direct funds set aside for education by the government to their children to a school of choice, whether the school is public, private or religious. In effect, separating the government financing of education from the government operation of schools.

Means-tested vouchers

Enabling income-eligible families, usually in limited numbers, to direct funds set aside for education by the government to pay for tuition at the public, private or religious school of their choice. *Examples*: Cleveland, Milwaukee

Failing schools vouchers

Allowing all parents whose children attend public schools identified as failing to direct funds set aside for education by the government to a better performing public, private or religious school of their choice. There are no income requirements, and eligibility is based solely on the success of individual public schools. *Examples*: Florida[16]

Although they are not strictly voucher systems, the states of Minnesota, Arizona, Iowa, and Illinois have developed tax credits or tax deductions on parents' state income taxes for certain educational expenses including transportation and tuition. Such programs do at least encourage parents to consider more seriously an educational option other than a public school.

Because the voucher system does allow public money to be used to attend religious schools, a major issue has been whether or not such plans are a violation of the First Amendment restriction of government passage of laws "respecting an establishment of religion, or prohibiting the free exercise thereof."[17] In June 2002, in the case of *Zelman v. Simmons-Harris*, the Court upheld the Cleveland plan which allowed students to receive a voucher to attend religious schools. Because plans differ, it is not safe to assume that every voucher program would be acceptable to the courts. A possible blow to allowing government funds for religious purposes came in a case before the Supreme Court in 2004. The Court's decision in *Locke v. Davey* prohibited the use of state scholarship money to students majoring in theology. Voucher opponents saw this decision as a positive sign for their position that the use of public money for religious schools was indeed a violation of the First Amendment.[18]

A plan for vouchers in Colorado has been held up by the state court, while in Washington D.C. a program has been established by Congress to allow "at least 1,700 low-income District children . . . to receive grants of up to $7,500 to attend private schools."[19] Both in Washington D.C. and in state capitals around the country, school vouchers have been a very partisan issue. The Republican Party has consistently supported the plans, while the Democrats along with the two major teacher unions, the National Education Association and the American Federation of Teachers, have strongly opposed the use of government funds for private schools. The National School Boards Association has publicly denounced the idea, citing a study of the Cleveland voucher system. This study concluded that "the evidence again proves that vouchers are not a miracle ticket to a better education. Once more, the realities of vouchers fail to live up to the promises. The one undeniable conclusion is that vouchers drain needed dollars from the public schools that educate most of America's students." In regard to academic achievement, the school board study claimed that in Cleveland "public school students, on average, made larger test score gains than students in the voucher program."[20]

Critics of vouchers have not only attempted to convince voters that academic achievement does not improve, but they also point out several other potential drawbacks with voucher plans:

- Any plan to give students a choice of schools can create transportation problems for either the parents or for the district.
- Under a voucher system, both public and private schools might spend significant amounts of money on advertising and recruiting. Neither of these activities results in improvements in the academic program.
- Because the most prestigious private schools would cost much more than any voucher, poor families still could not afford the most expensive private schools.
- Many wealthy parents who can afford the high tuition cost of some private schools would receive an unneeded government subsidy.
- Public schools would have to accept all students while private schools could be more selective. As a result, special education students and children with discipline problems would end up in the public schools, thus making them a "dumping ground" for difficult students.

Until recently, states that have allowed the voters a choice on vouchers have found that the majority of those participating in the referendums voted "No." Between 1972 and 2000, the voters in seven states turned down a voucher plan. In none of these states were the votes even close.[21]

Despite what has been an effective program to block the establishment of new voucher programs, there are signs that support might be growing at least among minority parents. Liberal African American columnist Clarence Page has written that desperate minority parents are becoming more supportive of vouchers as they lose faith in the public school systems. In a column written in March 2004, Page notes a 2002 poll that found that 57 percent of African American and 60 percent of Hispanic parents favored vouchers. In a 2004 episode of *The West Wing*, an award-winning political drama, the liberal Democratic president is convinced to sign a bill allowing a limited voucher system in the District of Columbia.[22]

Several factors will determine the future of vouchers and other choice programs. First and foremost will be the success of schools other than regular public schools in improving student academic achievement. Currently there is a lack of definitive research, and the results that have been published have been inconsistent. The second factor will be court decisions, especially at the Supreme Court level. It will be necessary for the Supreme Court to create some clearer guidelines regarding the church and state relationship for choice programs. Needless to say, the First Amendment will mean what the majority in the Supreme Court determines. With the Court now containing a number of older justices, the makeup and judicial philosophies of the members of the Court could change during the next several years. In our system, the political party that controls the presidency and the Senate will be in a position to choose justices whose views are in line with their party platforms. Politics will also affect the establishment of new choice programs at both the state and local level. As long as teachers' unions oppose vouchers and continue to provide significant support to the Democratic Party, there is likely to remain formidable opposition to voucher plans.

Even though they continue to oppose vouchers, a number of Democrats joined with the Republican majority in 2001 to pass the landmark education law known as the No Child Left Behind Act. A voucher plan endorsed by President Bush was not included in the final bill, but the law does allow the possibility of some parents receiving the right to choose a different school if their neighborhood school fails to improve test scores over a period of time. In addition, this legislation does place the federal government in the role of requiring schools to raise their academic standards. It is a law that undoubtedly took seriously the warnings and recommendations of the *A Nation at Risk* report. Its impact is just beginning to be felt, and it is to this legislation that we turn next.

NOTES

1. Kevin Ryan and James M. Cooper, *Kaleidoscope: Readings in Education* (Boston: Houghton Mifflin, 2004), 388.

2. Myra Pollack Sadker and David Miller Sadker, *Teachers, Schools, and Society* (Boston: McGraw-Hill, 2003), 167.

3. L. Dean Webb, Arlene Metha, and K. Forbis Jordan, *Foundation of American Education* (Upper Saddle River, NJ: Merril, 2000), 572.

4. Jack L. Nelson, Stuart B. Palonsky, and Mary Rose McCarthy, *Critical Issues in Education: Dialogues and Dialectics* (Boston: McGraw-Hill, 2004), 58.

5. Education Commission of the States, "Magnet Schools: Quick Facts," 2004, www.ecs.org/html/IssueSection.asp?issueid=80&s=Quick+Facts (accessed 7 March 2004), 1.

6. Education Commission of the States, "Magnet Schools: Pros and Cons," 2004, www.ecs.org/html/IssueSection.asp?issueid=80&s=Pros+%26+Cons (accessed 7 March 2004), 1.

7. Nelson, Palonsky, and McCarthy, *Critical Issues in Education*, 58.

8. Robert F. McNergny and Joanne M. Herbert, *Foundations of Education* (Boston: Allyn & Bacon, 1995), 547.

9. Alex Molnar, "Charter Schools: The Smiling Face of Disinvestment," *Educational Leadership*, 55, no. 2 (October 1996): 9–15.

10. Alan Richard, "The State of Charter Schools Nationwide," *Education Week*, 20 March 2002, www.iedx.org/article_1.asp?ContentID=EN520&SectionGroupID=NEWS (accessed 7 March 2004).

11. Sadker and Sadker, *Teachers, Schools, and Society*, 157.

12. Theodore Sizer, "Expert Critiques," *Public Agenda Online*, 1999, www.publicagenda.org/specials/learning/experts7.htm (accessed 25 February 2004), 3.

13. Diane Ravitch, "Expert Critiques," *Public Agenda Online*, 1999, www.publicagenda.org/specials/learning/experts5.htm (accessed 25 February 2004), 3.

14. Nelson, Palonsky, and McCarthy, *Critical Issues in Education*, 58–59.

15. David T. Gordon, ed., *A Nation Reformed?* (Cambridge, MA: Harvard Education Press, 2003), 12.

16. Milton & Rose D. Friedman Foundation, "Vouchers," *About School Choice*, 2002, www.friedmanfoundation.org/schoolchoice/index.html (accessed 7 March 2004), 1.

17. Walter Dean Burnham, *Democracy in the Making* (Englewood Cliffs, NJ: Prentice-Hall, 1983), 615.

18. Tony Mauro, "High Court Draws a Line on State-Funded Religion," *First Amendment Center*, 26 February 2004, www.firstamendmentcenter.org/analysis.aspx?id=12761 (accessed 7 March 2004), 1–2.

19. Spencer S. Hsu and Justin Blum, "D.C. School Vouchers Win Final Approval," *Washington Post*, 23 January 2004, www.washingtonpost.com/ac2/wpdyn?pagename=article&nide=&contentId=A4018 (accessed 7 March 2004), 1.

20. National School Boards Association, "Cleveland Study: Evidence Under-cuts Voucher Claims," 2003, www.nsba.org/site/doc.asp?TRACKID=&VID=2&CID=90&DID=32622 (accessed 8 January 2004), 1, 4.

21. National Education Association, "Voters Recently Reject Vouchers," www.nea.org/vouchers/vouchervotes.html (accessed 11 March 2004), 1.

22. Clarence Page, "Why Some Democrats Are Willing To Give School Vouchers a Break," *The Bata ia Daily News*, 6 March 2004, sec. A, p. 4.

CHAPTER 15

The Law

The No Child Left Behind (NCLB) legislation is a reauthorization of the Elementary and Secondary Education Act first passed in 1965 as part of President Lyndon B. Johnson's War on Poverty. It is evident to even a casual observer that the intentions of the law are quite consistent with many of the recommendations made in the *A Nation at Risk* report, but it took almost twenty years for the federal government to mandate the curriculum standards, high-stakes testing, and school accountability programs that we have today. Change was slow to occur under President Reagan's administration. His successor, George H. W. Bush, stimulated a reform initiative by calling together the state governors to establish a list of national educational objectives called Goals 2000. President Clinton, who was a leader in this effort as governor of Arkansas, adopted Goals 2000 when he assumed the presidency in 1993. Many of the ideas contained in the No Child Left Behind Act were included a year later in the Improving America's Schools Act, which was signed into law by President Clinton in 1994.[1]

George W. Bush came to the White House in 2001 with education as a major priority. It would take until January 8, 2002, to finally pass the No Child Left Behind Act. When it was finally signed into law, there was strong bipartisan support. The final version of the bill was passed 381 to 41 in the House of Representatives, and 87 to 10 in the Senate.[2]

The No Child Left Behind Act goes far beyond the earlier legislation in spelling out specific requirements and academic targets for all public school districts. An executive summary of the legislation, published by the Department of Education, lists the following aspects of the law:

- Increased accountability for states and school districts—Each state has been given the opportunity to develop challenging academic standards (what children must know and be able to do). To measure a school's success in achieving these standards, all students in grades three through eight must be tested annually in reading and math. "Assessment results and State progress objectives must be broken out by poverty, race, ethnicity, disability, and limited English proficiency to ensure that no group is left behind." Any school that is unable to make adequate yearly progress (AYP) will, over time, be required to provide corrective action.
- Greater choice for parents and students, particularly those attending low performing schools—Schools that are unable to meet State standards for at least three of the four preceding years are required to allow the parents of disadvantaged students to use the district's Title I allocations to pay for supplemental educational services chosen by the parents. These services can be provided by either a public or a private-sector provider.
- More flexibility for states and local educational agencies (LEA) in the use of federal education dollars—The bill gives "States and school districts unprecedented flexibility in the use of federal education funds in exchange for strong accountability for results."
- A stronger emphasis on reading, especially with our youngest children—A new Reading First grant program is included in the legislation. School districts that are successful in gaining one of these grants will use the money to assist children in grades K–3 who are at risk of reading failure. The grants also provide professional development opportunities in the field of reading instruction for teachers of grades K–3.
- New Improving Teacher Quality State Grants—These grants focus on providing assistance to schools in utilizing "scientifically based research to prepare, train, and recruit high-quality teachers."
- Assistance for states and local districts in providing safe, drug-free schools—"States must allow students who attend a persistently dangerous school or who are victims of violent crime at school to transfer to a safe school."[3]

This law, which appeared to be a great triumph for the Bush administration when it was passed, is emerging as a very controversial issue in the 2004 presidential election. As the implications of the new law began to become apparent in school districts across the country, the concerns of educators and politicians have multiplied. Typical of the issues being raised are the factors listed by the Program Evaluation Division of the State of Minnesota. This state agency concluded that although the goals of the law are positive, many school district superintendents believe that it is too "costly, unrealistic, and punitive." Education officials in Minnesota are worried about the requirement that students with disabilities and limited English skills are being held to the same achievement standards as all other students. The Program Evaluation Division also concluded that even if math and reading scores improve significantly, there will be a major increase in the number of schools failing to make "adequate yearly progress." In fact, they predicted that 80 percent of Minnesota elementary schools would not make the AYP by 2014. In addition, it was noted that the new costs created by the law might well exceed any new revenues coming to the schools.[4]

In March of 2004, fourteen states requested that the Federal Department of Education revise several of the regulations being used to enforce the law. They pointed out that "without any changes to the law, calculations suggest that within a few years, the vast majority of schools will be identified as in need of improvement." This will occur even if these schools have shown "steady and significant improvement for all groups of students." Officials in the Department of Education have responded by claiming that the changes being asked for cannot occur unless the law itself is changed. The chairman of the Education Committee in the House of Representatives, John A. Boehner, reacted harshly when he said that "these changes would gut the No Child Left Behind Act and make it easier for states to go back to hiding the fact that some children are being denied a quality education, even as those states accept billions in increased federal education funds."[5]

Representative Boehner mentions the money that will be forthcoming as a result of the law. It is the issue of having adequate financial resources to carry out the mandates of the No Child Left Behind Act that is worrying many educators. Our nation's largest teacher organization, the National Education Association, has publicly expressed the need for additional financial resources if schools are to have any chance of meeting the objectives of the new law. They have pointed out that the higher expectations being called for are coming at a time when "many states and local communities are still struggling with severe budget shortfalls and have cut back on instruction time or laid off quality teachers or school staff." In an article entitled "Cuts Leave More and More Public School Children Behind," a state-by-state listing is included of the cutbacks that are being made. Some examples of these budget reductions are listed below:

- In Alabama, it is expected that 4,000 teachers and 2,000 support personnel will be laid off. This is being done on top of the layoff of 2,000 teachers in each of the three previous years.
- In Florida, the state has cut the amount of learning that a student needs to receive a high school diploma in order to keep class sizes from increasing; students can now graduate by earning the bare minimum of eighteen credits in three years rather than twenty-four credits in four years.
- In Illinois, school districts across the state laid off thousands of teachers and support staff, leaving class sizes of nearly forty students in some schools.
- In Des Moines, Iowa, public school class sizes have grown from twenty-five to thirty-eight students.
- In Massachusetts, Boston has eliminated 1,000 positions, and more than 100 districts are charging fees for transportation and participation in sports.[6]

Organizations have been formed with the express purpose of overturning the law. One such group claims that the real purpose of the No Child Left Behind legislation is to undermine public education in the United States. For them, the plan is to place unrealistic demands on public schools and then provide too little support to meet these new demands. After labeling numerous schools as "failures," there will be sufficient support to introduce a major voucher system and to privatize education.[7]

In addition to very outspoken critics, the new law has already created a number of lawsuits. The Reading School District is suing the state of Pennsylvania, "which is responsible for enforcing the federal law, after seven of the district's schools were placed on the 'warning list' and six were placed on the more serious 'school improvement list' which allows students to demand transfers to attend better performing schools." A proposed law has been introduced in the Utah state legislature that would "direct the state to opt out of the federal NCLB law." If this were done, the state of Utah would lose 100 million dollars of Title I money.[8]

Another frequently heard criticism from administrators is the complexity of the legislation. It is claimed that "the law is so complicated that a small industry is popping up to work on it." It is providing new opportunities for lawyers and public relations firms. Larger districts are adding additional employees to coordinate NCLB compliance. There are numerous workshops being held for board members and administrators in an attempt to help educators understand the law.[9]

Although Republicans were hoping and expecting that the law would be considered one of their major accomplishments during President Bush's first term, polls have shown that many Americans are unfamiliar with the law. As the presidential campaign becomes more intense, Democrats, including Edward Kennedy, a supporter of the bill, are charging that President Bush has not kept his promises on funding. Senator Kennedy's friend and fellow senator from Massachusetts, John Kerry, the Democratic presidential candidate in the 2004 election, also voted for the bill. Kennedy is now pointing out in speeches that Congress authorized 18.5 billion dollars for Title I but that the budget President Bush sent to Congress included only 12.35 billion for this important federal program. Edward Kennedy has stated that "President Bush thinks he is providing enough for schools. Parents, teachers, and I don't."[10] Democrats go on to charge that the reason for the lack of funds is the growing federal deficit. This deficit, they believe, is being caused in large part because of the President's tax cuts, which many have suggested are primarily being given to the most affluent individuals in our society. The other economic factor affecting education is the weak economy, especially in certain regions of the country. In these areas, state governments, as well as local school districts, are having difficulty raising sufficient tax revenues to fund the programs necessary to meet the new federal expectations.

The debate has become heated, and the administration has begun to actively defend the law. One incident that has gained the headlines is a comment by Secretary of Education Rod Paige, in which he labeled the National Education Association as a "terrorist organization." Although

Secretary Paige later apologized for the comment, there remains a level of animosity between the teachers' unions and the administration.[11]

While it would appear that educational organizations throughout the nation are less than supportive of the No Child Left Behind Act as it is currently written, modifications in the enforcement have already been announced. Despite the evident opposition, there are many who believe that the law can have a positive impact on our schools. Bruce Fuller has written in the *Washington Post* that both parties are playing election year politics. "Instead of pulling together to revitalize schools, they're simply pummeling each other over this politically pivotal issue." While the critics have been outspoken, the administration also has been less than easy on those who have opposed the legislation. Secretary Paige is quoted as saying he "find[s] it staggering that the very critics . . . that fought so hard for civil rights could leave our African American, Hispanic American and special-needs children behind." After a study of the law at the University of California, Fuller concluded that if both sides would sit down together, there were "practical fixes" for those aspects of the legislation that were causing the most problems. It was his opinion that "both sides should ponder the fallout of fueling their inflammatory debate. Worn down by strident rhetoric and the uncertain local impact of NCLB, voters may grow skeptical of the government's ability to improve schools. Our children would be the big losers, especially those who remain left behind."[12]

There is little doubt that unless the two political parties can find common ground this well-intentioned law designed to bring about academic reform will fail. Already, public support for additional testing is waning. In a poll taken in 2003, two-thirds of the respondents "feared that the new emphasis on tests would lead to 'teaching to the test' and . . . three-fifths felt that this would be bad." A solution was put forward by James Traub in the *New York Times* when he wrote,

> I herewith propose a preemptive compromise. Liberal Democrats and teachers' unions and school professionals should stop trying to prove that No Child Left Behind is a failure and should stop pretending that money is the cure for everything; Republicans should accept that money does, however, matter terribly if you wish to attract the kind of teachers who can make a difference.[13]

In the meantime, he suggests that we must subject the law "to the kind of tinkering that incredibly complicated legislation generally requires."[14]

With the future of the No Child Left Behind Act still subject to political bickering, it is unlikely that major changes will occur prior to the 2004 election. With this uncertainty and also the question of the future of choice programs still being debated, the outcome of these major initiatives remains unclear. At any point in time, there will be unresolved factors that will affect the future, but it is necessary at this time to attempt to answer the question raised by the title of this book, *Are We Still A Nation At Risk Two Decades Later?*

NOTES

1. National Conference of State Legislatures, "No Child Left Behind Act of 2001," 2004, http://www.ncsl.org/programs/educ/NCLBHistory.htm (accessed 15 March 2004), 1.

2. National Conference of State Legislatures, "No Child Left Behind Act of 2001," 1.

3. U.S. Department of Education, "Executive Summary," January 2001, http://www.ed.gov/nclb/overview/intro/execsumm.html?exp=0 (accessed 19 March 2004), 1.

4. Minnesota Office of the Legislative Auditor, "No Child Left Behind," 26 February 2004, http://www.auditor.leg.state.mn.us/Ped/2004/0404sum.htm (accessed 15 March 2004), 1.

5. Diana Jean Schemo, "14 States Ask U.S. to Revise Some Education Law Rules," *New York Times*, 25 March 2004, http://www.nytimes.com/2004/03/25/education/25CHIL.html (accessed 25 March 2004), 1.

6. National Education Association, "Cuts Leave More and More Public School Children Behind," December 2003/January 2004, http://www.nea.org/esea/storiesfromthefield.html (accessed 15 March 2004), 1–23.

7. Jamie McKenzie, "The NCLB Wrecking Ball," *No Child Left.com*, November 2003, http://nochildleft.com/2003/nov03wrecking.html (accessed 15 March 2004), 1.

8. Internet Education Exchange, "NCLB Law Faces Challenges," http://www.iedx.org/article_1.asp?ContentID=EN755&SectionGroupID=NEWS (accessed 15 March 2004), 1.

9. Vincent L. Ferrandino and Gerald N. Tirozzi, "Getting Ahead of the No Child Left Behind," *National Association of Elementary School Principals*, 20 November 2002, http://www.naesp.org/ContentLoad.do?contentId=742 (accessed 6 January 2004), 1.

10. CNN.com, "Bush Makes Money, Touts Education," *Inside Politics*, 6 January 2004, http://www.cnn.com/2004/ALLPOLITICS/01/06/elec04.prez.bush.fundraising.ap/ (accessed 6 January 2004), 1–2.

11. Sam Dillon, "Education Chief Again Apologizes for 'Terrorist Remark,'" *New York Times*, 2 March 2004, http://www.nytimes.com/2004/03/02/politics/02PAIG.html (accessed 2 March 2004), 1.

12. Bruce Fuller, "No Politics Left Behind," *Washington National Weekly Edition*, 9–15 February 2004, 23.

13. James Traub, "True and False," *New York Times*, 21 December 2003, http://query.nytimes.com/gst/abstract.html?res=F50D12F93B580C728EDDAB0994DB404482 (accessed 6 January 2004), 1–2.

14. Traub, "True and False," 3.

CHAPTER 16

The Present

By calling their report *A Nation at Risk*, the authors were seeking to shock the reader and to initiate major reform in public education. This was undoubtedly the reason for the frequently quoted statement that "if an unfriendly foreign power had attempted to impose on America the mediocre educational performance that exists today, we might well have viewed it as an act of war. . . . We have, in effect, been committing an act of unthinking, unilateral educational disarmament."[1] Although the focus of the report is solely on education, the authors do acknowledge that schools are only one of the many reasons that our nation is at risk. Even so, the dramatic warning embodied in the Introduction did capture the attention of many people.

Prior to examining the success or failure of the efforts at educational reform during the past twenty years, it is important to consider the bigger question of whether the United States remains a nation at risk. In the early 1980s when the report was written, our economy was faltering, and we were losing whole industries to other countries. Our national debt was increasing, and many Americans were out of work. By the late 1990s, it seemed that the economy was doing well, and we had once again emerged as the world's great superpower. The new century has found us again with economic problems. Currently there are these statistics that are worrying many Americans:

- Despite longer hours and shorter vacations, American workers find that their wages are stagnant or declining, and employee benefits are being cut. U.S. businesses have remained cautious and slow to invest in new plants and new hires. When they do invest, the investment is often abroad. In recent years, U.S. companies have invested over seventy billion dollars in China alone.

- The manufacturing job base declined by 6 percent in 2003. Manufacturing job losses have continued for more than forty-three straight months. Since 2000, we have lost 2.5 million manufacturing jobs. The nation has also seen white-collar service jobs being moved out of the country.
- In 2002, 1.4 million more Americans fell below the federal poverty line, raising the number of poor to 34.8 million. Thirty million Americans earn less than $8.70 per hour. Real wages have fallen for a typical family by nearly $1,500 dollars a year.
- Household debt and government deficits are at record high levels. The federal debt is at $521 billion, and personal debt averages over $19,000 for each household for a total of two trillion dollars.[2]

Despite what seemed to be a dramatic upturn in the nineties, the nation now appears to have a number of serious economic problems. Many of these issues are caused at least in part by the extensive expenditures required by our current War on Terrorism. It would be difficult in 2004 to argue that we are not a nation at risk. The fact is that if history teaches anything, it is that all great powers rise and eventually fall. Thus, it is undoubtedly true that a powerful nation is always at risk of what would seem to be an inevitable decline. If every great power is always at risk of falling from its pinnacle, a more relevant question might be, are we better off than we were two decades ago? For the narrower purposes of this book, the question can be, are our schools better or worse than they were twenty years ago? Before considering the available data, it is important to note that the challenges facing public schools may have become more difficult during the past two decades. For instance, it is true that:

- Total enrollment in elementary and secondary schools has risen from approximately 40 million students to 46.7 million students.
- The number of students who speak a language other than English at home has more than doubled since 1979.
- There are at least 16 percent of our children ages five to seventeen who are living in poverty. At times during the last twenty years,

the percentage of poor children has been close to 20 percent. A child's home literacy environment varies by his or her poverty level. Poor children score lower than non-poor children on a home literacy index.

- Many more children are in single-parent homes, and 50 percent of the students in grades K–8 are involved in non-parental care arrangements after school.[3]

Realizing that the challenges may have been formidable, the results of the reform movement initiated by the *A Nation at Risk* report are, at best, mixed. Well-known educator John I. Goodlad believes that the report did have some positive impact. For him, the document stimulated "a surge of support from private philanthropy for innovative school improvement initiatives."[4] Theodore R. Sizer, a critic of many of our current reforms, has complimented the report on "its stark brevity, clear recommendations, particular focus on teenage youth, and, above all, its warlike rhetoric. . . ." Still, he has concluded that

most thoughtful people agree that the results so far have been disappointing. The reason is likely to be found less in the schools and to be largely due to the manner and settings (real and virtual) in which contemporary youths grow up, to the absence of influential adults regularly in their lives, and to the insistent and often engaging pressure of commerce-driven messages that surround them.[5]

A report entitled "Are We Still at Risk?," which was compiled by the Koret Task Force, agrees with Sizer's view that the results of the current reform movement have been less than impressive. The report includes the following criticisms:

- The Commission's diagnosis paid too little attention to the K–8 years and focused too heavily on high school.
- The report underestimated the resistance to change from the two largest teachers' unions, school administrators, schools of education, state bureaucracies, and school boards.
- The Commission also underestimated the significant number of Americans, particularly in middle-class suburbs, who believe their schools are basically sound and academically successful.[6]

This task force was not without hope as it pointed out that there were some reasons to be optimistic about the future. These included the continuing support for educational reform, especially among business leaders and elected officials. There is also a general acceptance of a standards-based curriculum. Finally, there is an increasingly angry and disenchanted feeling among minority parents that our inner-city schools are failing. This group is bound to become a more powerful lobby for reform. Still, in the Conclusion portion of the report, the authors give their opinion that during the past twenty years, we have "gained little by the way of better education results. Twenty years of entering first graders—about 80 million children—have walked into schools where they have scant chance of learning much more than the youngsters whose plight troubled the Commission in 1983."[7]

This rather pessimistic view does not take into account a number of changes that many would agree represent progress. Glenn T. Seaborg has traced the progress made on the recommendations of the *A Nation at Risk* report. In regard to curricular requirements, schools have added rigor to their curriculum but "their requirements still fall short" of those recommended by the Commission. The *A Nation at Risk* report also suggested that colleges and universities raise their expectations for admission. He reports that some colleges have done so and cites the University of California requirement that students take three years of science. Another recommendation called for longer school days or a lengthened school calendar. Longer school days are reported in 40 percent of the high schools, 30 percent of the middle schools, and 34 percent of the elementary schools across the country. Less than 20 percent of the schools have created longer school years, but additional homework is being given in over one quarter of the nation's schools.[8]

There were a number of recommendations that attempted to upgrade the teaching profession. Today, "teachers are tested in thirty-nine states as compared to only a handful of states in 1980." There are other examples of progress, but Seaborg concludes that "overall, the lack of progress in implementing the recommendations of the report, 'A Nation at Risk,' has been discouraging."[9]

The conclusions reached in the federal government publication *The Condition of Education 2003* were less critical of our nation's efforts at reform. In the view of the National Center for Educational Statistics, "trends in the condition of American education continued to show a mixed picture." They cite the following evidence:

- In reading, U.S. fourth-graders outscored their counterparts in many countries, and the percentages of high school graduates completing advanced-level courses in English have increased since the early 1980s. Yet the reading literacy scores of fifteen-year-olds in the United States were only average among industrial countries.
- In mathematics, the performance of fourth- and eighth-graders increased steadily throughout the 1990s, but the performance of twelfth-graders increased in the early part of the decade and then declined.[10]

The report also makes clear that the poverty level of students "sets the social context for their progress and achievement in school. Students from poor families do worse on tests than those from more affluent families."[11] The failure to solve the educational achievement problem in many of our schools that enroll primarily students from poor homes is perhaps the single most critical issue facing American education. It appears that

> we are recreating a dual school system, separate and unequal, almost half a century after it was declared unconstitutional. We face a widening and unacceptable chasm between good schools and bad, between those youngsters who get an adequate education and those who emerge from school barely able to read and write. Poor and minority children usually go to worse schools, have less expected of them, are taught by less knowledgeable teachers, and have the least power to alter bad situations. If we continue to sustain this chasm between the educational haves and have-nots, our nation will face cultural, moral and civic peril.[12]

As we look to the future it is to this dilemma that we must first turn.

NOTES

1. David T. Gordon, ed., *A Nation Reformed?* (Cambridge, MA: Harvard Education Press, 2003), 167.

2. Ben A. Franklin, ed., "Tightening Our Belts—A Major Issue in the 2004 Election Needs Explanation," *Washington Spectator*, 15 March 2004, 1–2.

3. Barbara Kridl, ed., *The Condition of Education 2003* (Washington D.C.: U.S. Department of Education, 2003), viii–x.

4. John I. Goodlad, "A Nation in Wait," *Education Week*, 23 April 2003, www.edweek.org/ew/ewstory.cfm?slug=32goodlad.h22 (accessed 16 December 2003), 4.

5. Theodore R. Sizer, "Two Reports," *Education Week*, 23 April 2003, www.edweek.org/ew/ewstory.cfm?slug=32sizer.h22 (accessed 16 December 2003), 1, 3.

6. Koret Task Force on K-12 Education, "Are We Still at Risk," *Education Next*, www.educationnext.org/20032/10.html (accessed 28 October 2003), 4–6.

7. Koret Task Force, "Are We Still at Risk?," 12.

8. Glenn Seaborg, "A Nation at Risk Revisited," www-ia1.lbl.gov/seaborg/risk.htm (accessed 29 August 2003), 2–3.

9. Seaborg, "A Nation at Risk Revisited," 6.

10. Barbara Kridl, ed., *The Condition of Education 2003*, x–xi.

11. Barbara Kridl, ed., *The Condition of Education 2003*, xi.

12. Educational Resources Information Center, "A Nation Still at Risk," *Eric Digests*, www.ericfacility.net/ericdigests/ed429988.html (accessed 6 October 2004).

CHAPTER 17

The Future

Even the most critical observer of American education would agree that we have many fine public schools. Some of these schools are located in poor urban neighborhoods as well as in remote, rural communities. Still, it is undoubtedly true that children living in affluent suburbs are most likely to have the opportunity to attend schools that are succeeding, especially if the measurement is the results of high-stakes tests. For this author, the problem of remedying these inequities of opportunity is our greatest educational challenge as a nation. This is true despite the fact that there are those who would suggest that money will not solve the problem even though educational spending is significantly higher per pupil in suburban districts than it is in communities that have low property values.

In an intriguing book entitled *Letters to the Next President*, a number of individuals with an interest in education have written a letter to the person who will be elected president in November 2004. Each of these letters gives the authors' opinions as to how the new administration can best deal with our nation's educational issues. Columbia education professor Thomas Sobol has addressed the issue of the need to spend money on poor schools with these words of advice:

> There are some areas where you need to spend money to improve the quality of schools and the education they provide. You can't reduce class size without hiring more teachers and using more space, and teachers and space cost money. You can't create new pre-school programs without hiring new staff, and hiring staff costs money. You can't expect teachers to teach the new curriculum effectively until they have mastered it, and

time for professional development costs money. Yet, reducing class size, making good pre-school programs available to all children, and providing teacher training have all been linked to improving student learning. The critics are right when they say that money alone will not solve our problems, but they need to understand that, while money on its own is not sufficient, it is necessary. The question is not whether we need more money; the question is how we can most effectively spend the money that we need.[1]

Professor Sobol has suggested that schools consider lowering class size, increasing preschool education, and providing additional teacher training as actions that are supported by valid research. For him and for others, spending money on such programs will help us to deal with what appears to be, in the words of Jonathan Kozol, the "savage inequalities" in our schools.

In regard to Sobol's first suggestion concerning class size, it has become part of the conventional wisdom in education that smaller classes are better for children. Most teachers, parents, and probably students would agree that when teachers have the opportunity to deal with fewer children, they are allowed to provide more individual attention to each child. At the same time, teachers would also claim that classroom management is much easier with fewer students. Historically, although there have been fluctuations in average class sizes, the long-term trend has been to have less students in classes. Economic conditions in the country, state, or region can also affect how many students will be in the classrooms of our schools. When money is tight, class size tends to increase.

Although there has been a good deal of research on the educational effect of smaller classes, the most comprehensive and influential study was the Tennessee Project STAR (Student Teacher Achievement Ratio), which occurred in the 1980s. This long-range study showed that in grades K–3 reducing class size from twenty-five to fifteen had positive impacts on the students in smaller classes. Because of this and other studies, states and individual school districts have embarked on class size reduction programs. In California, lowering class size has become the major component of the state's concerted efforts to raise test scores. Of course there are critics of this approach, but it continues to be a strategy that is generally accepted in public education. Because of the cost of hiring new teachers and often providing additional classrooms, it is an extremely expensive reform. With the growing federal deficit along with the economic problems of many state governments, the trend toward reduction of class size has actually been reversed in a number of school districts. Even so, the findings of the STAR study remain a powerful influence in the current educational reform movement. One scholar who studied the research on class size found that

> the effect of small classes grew stronger as children spent more years in them. Students who spent four years in small classes gained approximately twice as much as did children who spent just one year. In high school, the children who had been in small classes continued to do better on a variety of standardized tests than did the children from regular classes. They were less likely to drop out of school, more likely to graduate from high school on time, and more likely to take advanced courses, earn high grades, and go to college. The longer the children from small classes are followed, the more impressive their outcomes seem.[2]

Project STAR also strongly suggests that although small classes will help all children, they will have the most positive impact on disadvantaged children. If one wishes to believe our best educational research, it would indicate that reducing class size should continue to be one of the reforms that is pursued in order to improve all schools, but especially those where there are students who have the greatest need. Still, it is true that without highly motivated and well-trained teachers, the investment in lower class sizes will largely be wasted.

To ensure that other reforms are effective, we must focus on the area of teacher training. Like the reduction of class size, there is a general agreement in the United States that the single most important factor in ensuring the success of any school is the teacher in the classroom. The importance of this fact is supported not only by public opinion but by research. The work of Linda Darling-Hammond suggests that "the best way to improve school effectiveness is by investing in teacher training. Stronger teaching skills and qualifications lead to greater student learning."[3]

The first step in attempting to improve the quality of teachers is to attempt to recruit more outstanding people to the profession. We must find talented individuals both from the traditional students who enter college directly from high school and also those people who might make a decision to pursue teaching after working in other careers. Because of the cost of preparing to become a teacher, scholarships for highly qualified candidates in both groups are one tactic that might cause additional candidates to consider the profession. For others, an increase in teacher salaries might help to make teaching a more inviting career choice.

Recruiting the right type of individual is only part of the problem. The *A Nation at Risk* report also called for opportunities for advancement within the profession. So-called career ladders allow teachers to gain promotions within the teaching ranks. Similar to the various levels used in most colleges, teachers would be able to earn increasingly more respect and additional salary as they are promoted within the district.

We must also seek to stem the attrition rate of new teachers, especially the large numbers leaving our most troubled schools. Matching a new teacher with a seasoned classroom veteran has in many cases been helpful. These so-called mentor teachers must be carefully chosen and trained for their positions. If this is done, they can help new teachers through those very difficult first three years in the classroom.

Finally, we must do a better job ensuring that new teachers continue to grow professionally. This cannot be done by merely offering three unrelated conference days or workshops each year. Teachers, like other professionals, need to have an ongoing training program that includes in-depth involvement in the issues they are facing in their daily work. The occasional motivational speaker might have a temporary inspirational effect, but such speakers are no substitute for a true professional growth program. Like class size, investing in attempting to improve the quality of professional practices of classroom teachers, if done correctly, is a reform that has been validated by research.

The same can be said about efforts to provide outstanding school leaders. Numerous studies have pointed to the importance of principals in developing high-achieving schools.[4] Just as we must find the right people to become our classroom teachers, school districts must encourage employees with leadership potential to consider a career as a school administrator. Currently, it would seem that we are facing a problem in this regard. To ensure that our schools have the best administrators possible, boards of education might consider programs that would assist future leaders financially as they seek to gain administrative certification. Schools of education must do a much better job preparing future leaders. Field-based programs with realistic internships are necessary. As with teachers, new administrators can benefit from having a mentor after assuming their first leadership position.

Improved leadership is also necessary from our local boards of education. Individuals who are motivated to serve all of the children in their district must be willing to step forward. Instead of single-issue candidates, we need talented and positively motivated leaders who are willing to represent their community and to work with teachers and administrators to improve the schools for all children. Real progress will come most easily to districts where the board of education and the employees of the district make the welfare of students their primary concern.

One additional reform that boards of education might consider in larger districts is the possibility of creating smaller school organizations. Even in large buildings, it is possible to organize "schools within a school." It now seems clear that a team of teachers working with 100 to 150 students in a secondary school can provide a more personal and academically supportive environment for students. Despite the fact that for more than a century we have been creating larger and larger school districts, "research suggests that small schools are more effective at every educational level, but they may be most important for older students."[5]

For children who have yet to begin school, there now appears to be sufficient positive research to support new efforts to provide preschool education (programs for students ages three and four). Since the inception of the Head Start program in 1965, we have had an ongoing national debate concerning the value of preschool education. Head Start was a part of President Lyndon B. Johnson's War on Poverty, and it was established to give a boost to children from disadvantaged homes and allow them to be competitive with students from more affluent homes when they began kindergarten. Like other parts of the poverty program, its funding was negatively affected by the cost of the war in Vietnam and the less-than-enthusiastic support of several presidential administrations, beginning with Richard Nixon. At the same time that fewer poor children were being enrolled in Head Start, many more affluent parents sought private programs, either because of their educational value or as a place to send their children rather than a more traditional day care facility. As the number of working mothers increased in the 80s and 90s, private preschool programs grew rapidly. While this was occurring, the growth of Head Start was being negatively affected by some early studies that questioned its effectiveness. By the late 1970s, though, there was research that began to show positive results for the program, and by the mid-1980s, there was "some direct evidence" that Head Start was having positive effects on the children who attended the programs. Because of the comprehensive nature of Head Start, some of these positive outcomes went beyond the academic results. Students attending had better nutrition and health and were more likely to have been immunized. There was also evidence that children in the program adjusted better to school, had fewer absences, and were less likely to be held back. Even with these positive results, in 1988, only 16 percent of those children eligible were enrolled in Head Start programs.[6]

Perhaps because of a number of favorable studies, both President George H. W. Bush and Bill Clinton were able to convince Congress to increase funding for Head Start. During the 1990s, there were again a number of criticisms of the program, and it became clear that not all of the centers were of equal quality. This was true because of low wages, as many employees of the program were paid salaries that were not competitive enough to recruit well-prepared staff. While Head Start programs were being debated, additional studies were conducted showing that private programs were making a difference for children. As a result of his study of the evidence concerning all preschool education programs, Timothy H. Hasci concluded that preschool education "does some good, and that if government continues to focus on improving the quality of Head Start programs, it will do more good." His final words on Head Start are that "if we are truly concerned with educating disadvantaged children, one significant step would be to make sure there are places for all in high-quality preschool classrooms."[7]

A final research-based priority, as noted earlier, would be an ongoing effort to engage parents in the education of their children. This is undoubtedly best accomplished at the local level, but creative initiatives by school districts could be supported by state or federal funding. Increased parental involvement is also perhaps one of the best ways to affect the problem of poor student motivation. Additional steps such as reducing the amount of time students can work outside of school and support for more positive recognition of students who achieve academic success will only occur in schools where parents work with teachers and administrators to change a number of the current priorities in the lives of our young people.

Significant funding for any of the initiatives mentioned in this chapter is unlikely to come from local sources. This is especially true if school districts must continue to rely primarily on property taxes to supply the local share of the school budget. Poor districts are not in a position to raise sufficient funds to initiate preschool option policies or class-size reduction programs. It is also true that the potential of state governments to raise money for education varies greatly. Relying on the governors and state legislatures to achieve equal education opportunity even within their own states has failed. Expecting court decisions to force a more equitable distribution of state aid has yet to solve the problem in many states. If one accepts the premise that the single most pressing national education problem is our failure to educate properly our most economically disadvantaged children, it is difficult to escape the conclusion that the only viable solution is more active federal government participation in a concerted effort to equalize educational opportunity. Linda Darling-Hammond has written that

> for the cost of one percent of the Bush administration's tax cuts in 2003 or the equivalent of one week's combat cost during the war in Iraq, we could provide top-quality preparation for more than 150,000 new teachers to teach in high-need schools and mentor all the new teachers who are hired over the next 5 years. With just a bit of focus and a purposeful plan, we could ensure that all students in the United States are taught by highly qualified teachers within the next 5 years. Now that would be real accountability to children and their parents.[8]

Even doubling the federal contribution would still have Washington providing only about 15 percent of the total revenue being used to support public schools. The fear of conservatives is that if the federal government goes beyond its current spending level on public education it will somehow gradually bring about the federal takeover of our schools. This would of course be a major change from our historic reliance on state and local control. Congress grappled with this issue when it finally agreed on the provisions of the No Child Left Behind legislation. In its final form, the law gave to the states the job of developing standards and tests to evaluate academic progress. The federal government merely set up the ground rules for continued federal financial assistance. As the presidential campaign heats up, the fight over whether more money should come from Washington continues. Prominent Democrats such as Senator Edward Kennedy have labeled President Bush's funding proposals for education "a tin cup budget." Kennedy has gone on to charge that President Bush "misstated, misspoke, misrepresented his position" on financing No Child Left Behind. The importance of this issue is highlighted by the fact that

> a recent poll by *Education Week* and the Public Education Network ranked education second in the list of voter concerns behind only the economy, and ahead of terrorism, security, health care, prescription drugs, and the wars in Afghanistan and Iraq. And 60 percent of those polled said that the federal government did not contribute enough money to public schools.[9]

Even if voter pressure causes Congress to appropriate more money for education, the question becomes how should this money be spent? Thus far, I've suggested that the wisest priorities for raising academic achievement would be major financing of programs in schools that deal primarily with disadvantaged students. These programs would include funds that would allow for:

- Reducing class size, especially in grades K–3
- Establishing smaller school organizations within large districts
- Providing sufficient funding to allow all eligible preschool children to attend improved Head Start programs
- Scholarships and other funding of programs to induce excellent people to consider teaching in high need districts and support for staff development and mentoring programs for all teachers
- Assistance to school districts in developing innovative approaches to involving parents in their children's education. These proposals can help to make schools an even more important part of every community. We could certainly improve our school districts if the school buildings and the houses of worship became the gathering centers and sources of pride of citizens rather than the malls, the gambling parlors, or the athletic stadiums. Money should be available to allow school districts to rehabilitate their decaying buildings, or if necessary, build new ones.
- As a nation, we must continue to seek to draw more of our "best and brightest" people into the teaching profession. Money is only one of the ways to accomplish this, but it is a necessary component.

- Finally, positive leadership is necessary. We must have articulate and committed people at every level of government, who can gain the necessary public support to bring about change. The president, Congress, as well as governors and state legislatures, must make education a top priority. Even if this occurs, lasting reform will not be successful unless the leadership at all levels is able to agree upon the nature of the reforms and work together to implement them.

While the above priorities do provide ways to proceed, there will be other agendas offered. During the 1990s, huge amounts of money were spent on educational technology. Because most citizens were seeing the impact of computers in their own lives, boards of education and school administrators had little trouble gaining support for spending on technology. Too often, districts made errors in how they used this money. Districts quickly made major investments in computer hardware and software without developing careful long-range plans for the uses of educational technology. Not enough money was spent in many districts on either training teachers or providing the necessary staffing to maintain the systems. Some districts also failed to think about the rapid obsolescence of their equipment. The result has been that many schools have not achieved the academic results that might have been possible. Computers sit idly in some classrooms and are not used in others because they are in need of repair. In still other classrooms, we have teachers who either are clueless on how to use the technology or who actually are resisting pressures to integrate it into their teaching.

In a book by William D. Pflaum entitled *The Technology Fix*, the author lists the bold promises that many accepted concerning the benefits of educational technology. The dream was that we would accomplish the following:

- Schools would create student-centered classrooms, where computers that tailored instruction to the individual needs of every learner would replace the teacher-centered classroom.
- Students would no longer be passive recipients of information. Technology would empower them to become active participants in the construction of their own knowledge. With access to the world's ever-expanding pool of knowledge, . . . the classroom would become the world.

- Skills would not be neglected. Engaging multimedia programs would adapt to each student's learning style. . . . Static textbooks would gather dust, replaced by dynamic, always-up-to-date learning resources.
- Computer technology would revolutionize the classroom structure. Teachers would learn alongside their students. They would be facilitators of student self-learning, not purveyors of a one-size-fits-all curriculum. Test scores would soar, or tests would disappear altogether.

After a year-long study of how computers are being used in the classroom, Pflaum concluded that although the above benefits represented the potential promise of technology, "the reality, so far, has fallen short. . . . Technology's bold promises have been broken."[10]

Even supporters of placing numerous computers in each classroom agree that the initiative is still "a gamble" and that "relatively little evidence backs the idea that computers improve learning in readily measurable ways."[11] In fact, a study conducted by Joshua Angrist and Victor Lavy concluded that computer-assisted instruction "does not appear to have had educational benefits that translated into higher test scores."[12] Even if one could prove that computers truly enhance learning, we still have the problem that poorer schools have fewer computers than do schools in more affluent communities. It is also true that the students in the disadvantaged schools are much less likely to have a home computer to enhance their learning. In any case, while it would be unwise to give up on computers as an educational tool, it is an initiative that requires considerable planning. In many communities it would be helpful to pause in the technology initiative long enough to carefully plan how computers can truly improve learning. In the meantime, there are enough research-based programs to finance with any additional revenue that might be forthcoming.

If districts should be cautious about major new spending on technology, they also should carefully consider the wisdom of another proposed answer to our educational problems. Just as technology has yet to prove its long-term educational value, school choice remains a controversial direction for the future. Continued experimentation with magnet schools, open enrollment, and charter schools can perhaps be justified, but moving to a total voucher system at this time could be a questionable strategy. This is especially true if we rely heavily on the so-called educational management organizations (EMOs) to provide alternatives to public schools. We would be doing so "despite the fact that the track record of Edison and other corporate EMOs is educationally and economically dismal."[13]

Edison, which is the best-known and largest of the EMOs, saw investor confidence plummet in 2002 as its stock went from a high of thirty-seven dollars a share to as low as fourteen cents a share. *The Nation* magazine reported that the company was saved from collapse by a 182 million dollar infusion of funds by the Florida Retirement System, which represents, among other public employees, Florida's public school teachers. A number of public employees, legislators, and "several prominent newspapers criticized the deal, suggesting unsavory political motives." Despite this investment, Edison continues to have heavy costs for marketing and a number of very highly paid managers. The magazine notes that the company is still losing money even though they are being paid a higher amount for each student than the public schools in the same community receive. In regard to their educational success, a study by professor Gary Maron concluded that, in comparison with public schools in the same district, "they are doing similarly or slightly worse."[14]

Because there is not yet any comprehensive research on the few voucher experiments that are taking place, it would seem that, like technology, we should as a nation move very slowly in the implementation of this proposed innovation. Public schools in the United States have existed for over 150 years and for the most part have been successful in helping to make us a great nation. We need to be careful about dismantling this very important American institution.

As we look to the future, perhaps the most important change that could occur would be if we could make our public schools our primary national priority. To do this, education must once again be put in the spotlight. This was accomplished in 1983 by the *A Nation at Risk* report. The changes that have occurred because of the report have in part been positive, but there is no doubt that the issues raised in 1983 have not been resolved two decades later. It is time for a new generation of leaders to take a turn at attempting to revitalize our nation's schools. Currently we are launched on an agenda that relies on curriculum standards, high-stakes testing, and accountability as mandated by the No Child

Left Behind legislation. These initiatives alone will not transform our schools. At the same time, we cannot depend on merely spending more money to achieve our objectives. Still, those who oppose spending money, especially on the schools of underprivileged children should

> look at the facilities, curriculum, materials, teacher-pupil ratio and number and quality of educators in the schools that they send their own children to and then compare it to the crumbling buildings, inadequate ventilation, scarcity of textbooks, and the lack of stability and quality of the personnel in America's poorest schools.[15]

If we wish to make the twenty-first century a second "American Century," we must ensure that our schools provide for the nation an intelligent, informed citizenry along with a new group of wise leaders. We are not doing that badly. At the elementary level, reading and math scores are improving; at the secondary level, dropout rates are declining, and more students are going on to higher education. We cannot deny the fact that the progress during the past twenty years has been uneven and slow. Despite spending more on education, we continue to have extremely unequal schools. "UNICEF [United Nations International Children's Emergency Fund] ranks the equality of United States education an abysmal 21st out of 24 industrial countries. . . . Twenty-five of our nation's state Supreme Courts have said our educational funding systems are inequitable or inadequate." More to our shame, the United Nations reports that we rank "21st out of 22 developed countries in the percent of children in poverty."[16]

In 1832, Abraham Lincoln in his first public political speech said "upon the subject of education, not presuming to dictate any plan or system respecting it, I can only say that I view it as the most important subject which we as a people can be engaged in."[17] If as a nation we can adopt Lincoln's view, the twenty-first century will be a better time, not only for us, but for the world. By accomplishing this as a society, we might well be able to escape, at least for a time, the label of a nation at risk.

NOTES

1. Carl Glickman, ed., *Letters to the Next President* (New York: Teacher's College Press, 2004), 195–96.

2. Timothy A. Hacsi, *Children as Pawns* (Cambridge, MA: Harvard University Press, 2003), 119–20.

3. Myra Pollack Sadker and David Miller Sadker, *Teachers, Schools, and Society* (Boston: McGraw-Hill, 2003), 212.

4. Sadker and Sadker, *Teachers, Schools, and Society*, 201.

5. Sadker and Sadker, *Teachers, Schools, and Society*, 210.

6. Hacsi, *Children as Pawns*, 44.

7. Hacsi, *Children as Pawns*, 60–61.

8. Hacsi, *Children as Pawns*, 253.

9. Diana Jean Schemo, "Kennedy Demands Full Funding for School Bill," *New York Times*, 7 April 2004, www.nytimes.com/2004/04/07/education/07kennedy.html (accessed 7 April 2004), 2.

10. William D. Pflaum, "The Technology Fix: The Promise and Reality of Computers in Our Schools," *Association for Supervision and Curriculum Development*, www.ascd.org/publications/books/104002/intro.html (accessed 4 March 2004), 2.

11. Evan Hansen, "Public Schools: Why Johnny Can't Blog," *CNET News.com*, 12 November 2003, http://news.com.com/2009-1023-5103805.html (accessed 6 February 2004), 2.

12. Hansen, "Public Schools: Why Johnny Can't Blog," 3.

13. Evans Clinchy, "Reimaging Public Education," *Phi Delta Kappan*, February 2004, 449.

14. David Moberg, "How Edison Survived," *The Nation*, 15 March 2004, 22–23.

15. Carl Glickman, ed., *Letters to the Next President*, 5.

16. Carl Glickman, ed., *Letters to the Next President*, 49.

17. Abraham Lincoln, "Abraham Lincoln Quotes and Quotations," www.topicsites.com/abraham-lincoln/quotes.htm (accessed 7 April 2004).

Index

National Association for Alternative Certification. *See* teachers

National Board Certification, 80–81

National Board for Professional Teaching Standards, 40

National Commission on Excellence in Education, 47; certification of teachers, 81–82; establishment of, 7–9, 12; Gardner, David Pierpont, 16–18; Letter of Transmittal, 16–17; meetings and public events of, 15; members, 12–14; mission statement of, 14–15; priorities of, 15–16. *See also* Bell, Terrel; *A Nation at Risk* report; schools

National Council for the Accreditation of Teacher Education, 82

National Council on Education, 76

National Education Association, 160, 162

National Institute to Education. *See* teachers

National Research Council. *See* funding, educational

National Teacher Examination. *See* teachers

NCATE. *See* National Council for the Accreditation of Teacher Education

NCLB. *See* No Child Left Behind Act

"New Basics." *See* curriculum

No Child Left Behind Act, 62, 71, 99, 108, 155, 158–64, 178–79, 182–83; adequate yearly progress (AYP) 159–60; criticisms of, 161, 163

NTE. *See* National Teacher Examination

open enrollment, 149

Paideia Proposal. See "back to basics"

Parent Teacher Association, 6, 118, 121

parents: communication with, 122–23; engaged in education of children, 177, 179; involvement and responsibility of, 115–21. *See also A Nation at Risk* report

performance-based salaries. *See* teachers

preschool education. *See* Head Start

principals, 70, 102–3, 143, 175; high turnover rate, 104; leadership, improved, 104, 176; retirement of, 104. *See also A Nation at Risk* report

Project STAR. *See* schools

PTA. *See* Parent Teacher Association

Public Law 94-142. *See* Education for All Handicapped Children Act

Ravitch, Diane, vii, 2, 46, 54, 117

Reading First grant program, 159

Reagan, Ronald, 1, 2, 6–7, 18, 134–35

reform movement, as a result of *A Nation at Risk* report: challenges, 167–68, 172; Koret Task Force report, 168–69; mixed results, 168–69; National Center for Educational Statistics, 169–70; necessary changes needed for, 172–80; Sobol, Thomas, 172–73; still at risk, 168–69. *See also* economy; Goals 2000

Rodriquez v. San Antonio. *See* funding, educational

About the Author

William Hayes has been a high school social studies teacher, department chair, assistant principal, and high school principal. From 1973 to 1994, he served as superintendent of schools for the Byron-Bergen Central School District, which is located eighteen miles west of Rochester, New York. During his career he was an active member of the New York State Council of Superintendents and is the author of a council publication entitled *The Superintendency: Thoughts for New Superintendents*, which is used to prepare new superintendents in New York State.

Mr. Hayes has also written a number of articles for various educational journals. After retiring from the superintendency, he served as chair of the Teacher Education Division at Roberts Wesleyan College in Rochester, New York, until 2003. He currently remains a full-time teacher at Roberts Wesleyan. During the past five years he has written seven books, all of which have been published by ScarecrowEducation. They include *Real-Life Case Studies for School Administrators* (2000), *Real-Life Case Studies for Teachers* (2000), *So You Want to Be a Superintendent?* (2001), *So You Want to Be a School Board Member?* (2001), *Real-Life Case Studies for School Board Members* (2002), *So You Want to Be a College Professor?* (2003), and *So You Want to Be a Principal?* (2004).